THE ITALIAN CHAPEL, ORKNEY

Donald S. Murray is a teacher, author and journalist whose poetry, prose and verse has been shortlisted for both the Saltire Award and Callum Macdonald Memorial Award. He has also been awarded the Jessie Kesson Fellowship and the Robert Louis Stevenson Fellowship. As well as a number of his books having been chosen as Books of the Year by *The Guardian*, his Gaelic play *Sequamur* was also a success, performed at various venues throughout these islands, as well as Ypres in Belgium. He is the author of *SY StorY: A Portrait of Stornoway Harbour* and *The Guga Hunters*, also published by Birlinn.

THE
ITALIAN
CHAPEL
ORKNEY

DONALD S. MURRAY

Donald S Murray
7/8/18

BIRLINN

Published in 2017 by
Birlinn Limited
West Newington House
10 Newington Road
Edinburgh
EH9 1QS

www.birlinn.co.uk

First published in 2010 as *And On This Rock*

ISBN 978 1 78027 429 4

British Library Cataloguing-in-Publication Data
A catalogue record for this book is available from the British Library

Designed and typeset by Edderston Book Design, Peebles
Printed and bound by Grafica Veneta, Italy

To the Chiocchetti family,
Fabio, Letizia and Angela,
and also Nathan Hunter Smith,
part of the future of Orkney.

CONTENTS

LIST OF ILLUSTRATIONS

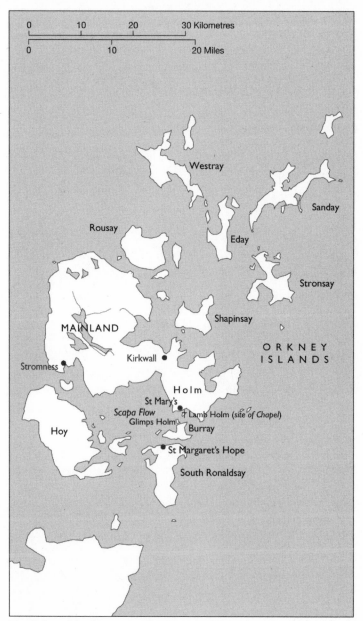

The Orkney Islands

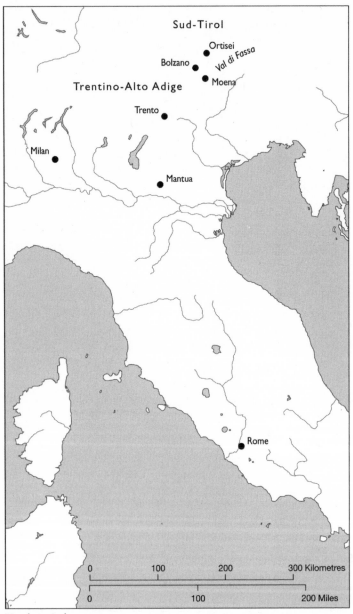

Northern Italy

'*Empea n lumin e no maledir el scur.*'
'Far better to light a candle than forever curse the darkness.'

Ladin inscription on the family home of
Domenico Chiocchetti

'What a strange scene you describe and what strange prisoners. They are just like us.'

Plato, *The Republic*, Book VII

1

AND ON THIS ROCK . . .

Once upon a time, there was . . .

'A king!' my little readers will say at once.

No, children, you're wrong. Once upon a time, there was a group of Italian prisoners who were held captive on an island in the far north. They spent St Lucy's Day – the winter solstice – mourning that they were trapped in a place where man's vision is at its most narrow and limited at a time when the sun is spent and sky and sea blur together. They would stand at the most southerly end of the island which those who guarded them called the Mainland of Orkney and look out at all the other islands to their south, Lamb Holm, Glimps Holm, Burray, South Ronaldsay, finding it hard to distinguish them from the greyness of the rest of the horizon. Land was dim and bleary, its solidity seemed insubstantial and intangible, a creation of the mist and shadows that loomed all round.

It was the sea they noticed most. Its fierceness seemed ready to devour them, rock and hillock, shoreline and sand. After the relative calm of summer, it looked as if it had been transformed into a white-maned dragon, prepared to swallow all that came in its path. Man himself seemed weak in comparison with its force and power, a frail St George with only a fist to wave hopelessly in its direction. It would take more than his strongest lance to turn its power back.

And so these prisoners, trapped there in January 1942, prayed for relief from the fury of the elements. Barely able to see as they walked these shores, bowed by the onslaught of salt and wind, they said a few prayers to St Lucy, patron saint of the blind. They called upon other saints, too, to intercede for them. St Andrew, the patron saint of the fishermen they sometimes saw out in their boats, the saint of the new country to which they had come. St George, the patron saint of soldiers. St Leonard, the patron saint of prisoners. St Jude the Apostle, the help for the hopeless, to whom they must have prayed time and time again as they looked around the island where they were incarcerated.

'*Eloi, Eloi, lama sabachthani?*' they would have asked, echoing the words of the Mass. 'My God, my God, why have you forsaken me?'

Others provided comfort for themselves by thinking of the childhood stories they had heard from their friends and neighbours, mothers and fathers. They recalled the folk tales they had heard. One or two might have remembered Carlo Collodi's tale of the puppet-boy, *Pinocchio*, a book they had discovered in their childhood when they sat in their classroom or clustered around a parent's knee. If they did, they, perhaps, mouthed words from its opening chapter, how Master Cherry the carpenter had lifted up his hatchet to start trimming down a log of wood. He was just about to strike his first blow when he heard the log speak.

'Don't hit me too hard!'

Yet life had sometimes done that to them, dealing out heavy blows, especially over the years of war. Some recalled how their mouths had hung open, the wonder and horror they felt when, as children, they were just about to embark upon a magical journey into the puppet-boy's life. He, too, had left his home with all its comforts to embark on a magical adventure. He, too, had suffered a thousand tricks, deceits and humiliations on his journey until he returned once more to his father's love. They hoped that the same might happen to them, that some day they might be able to go back home, take off their prison uniforms and have their humanity restored to them once more.

And so they prayed for a miracle, one that would restore their hope and faith in the grace of God, the presence of angels, trusting that some day their sense of themselves as individuals, real and breathing people, might return . . .

2

FOUNDATIONS

LAMBHOLM WALTZ

Salt savages the kisses
of each Lambholm storm
as she swirls around these prisoners,
never giving warmth
to these men who dream of partners
once held tightly in their arms,
dark Rosella in the tarantella,
Angelina in the waltz.

Yet still they practise dance-steps,
half-forgotten harmonies
with imaginary partners pictured
within that island's boundaries,
those fixed by rules and regulations,
or laid down by beat of wind or sea,
defying them by humming waltz or tarantella,

'Rosella, Angelina, une, due, tre . . .'

'It was only for the first year or so of the war,' Archie Wylie declares as we sit together in a small cottage in Holm at the southern end of the Orkney mainland, 'but there's no doubt that for a wee while, Orkney was in the front line. No doubt about it at all.'

He stretches out his hands as he recalls what it was like to be a young boy in the Kirkwall of these years. From time to time, he chuckles, his broad head – almost bald, apart from his grey temples and a few wisps of hair standing upright at its centre – nodding with amusement. His face lightens at the recklessness he displayed back then, eyes sparkling behind his glasses. 'I remember the fuel tank near the town going up. I remember being in school one day and watching the German planes coming over, dropping their bombs on the island. There used to be our guns, too, firing at them, trying to stop them. I wasn't scared of it at all. I must admit I used to really enjoy it . . .'

Looking out his window at the quietness of the scene outside these days, it would be easy for me to convince myself that Archie was making this all up, a product, perhaps, of years dreaming at the wheel of his Co-op van as he took groceries to the good people of Burray and South Ronaldsay. But there is something in the heartiness of the man's voice, his sheer solidity and bulk that impresses and gives conviction to his words.

There is also the testimony of Dorothy Rendall, sitting at the other side of the fire, talking about the bombs landing on the foreshore of Holm, a short distance from the cottage that at one time also served as one of the local shops. 'Were you not scared?' she mutters, 'There's no doubt I was. I used to hide away and keep my eyes shut until it was all over.'

The books provide their own evidence of the reasons why it might have been more sensible for young Archie to have done the same. In *Gas Masks And Ration Books*, local historian G.L. Esson notes that 'air raids were frequent during the early part of the war' on Orkney as a whole 'and South Ronaldsay and Burray were bombed several times.' He outlines how a number of these incidents took place not far from the cottage where Archie and

Dorothy sat that day in April when I spoke with them. There was the moment the farmhouse of Ladywater in Burray suffered damage when a landmine exploded nearby. A civilian was injured, too, after the Luftwaffe dropped a series of bombs on an army hut and a farmhouse in Deerness. Young, red-headed Dorothy must have kept her head down and screwed her eyes tight shut the day an enemy aircraft dropped some twenty bombs in a line from Widewall to St Margaret's Hope, doing her best to pretend that all these blasts and explosions were not disrupting the peace of her world.

Yet it would have difficult for anyone in Orkney to do this for long. Houses like Graemeshall, looking out on Lamb Holm, had their windows blown in. Corpses were occasionally washed up on the shore, reminders of the reality of men 'lost at sea'. There was suddenly a population of 60,000 on the island, as opposed to the 20,000 living there before the war. At no time was the pretence less possible than in the days and weeks following the moment the HMS *Royal Oak* was sunk in Scapa Flow. It was an event that occurred on 14 October 1939 when the German U-boat *U-47* sneaked through Kirk Sound, the narrow stretch of water between the village of St Mary's and Lamb Holm, threading its way through the sunken merchant-ships designed to prevent the enemy entering the waters of that largely landlocked bay. Once the twists and turns of this journey were complete, it found itself in a sheltered, north-eastern corner of the anchorage, its periscope turning in the direction of one of Britain's most legendary battleships. The *Royal Oak* was positioned to protect the important RDF station at Netherbutton near Kirkwall, its anti-aircraft guns bristling to prevent any airborne assault on the building. It was not, however, prepared for any attack from sea. Its men had not yet become accustomed to the grim routine of a war which had only just begun. Useful in the First World War, their vessel was now only fit for second-line duties as opposed to the full hurly-burly of armed conflict. And these attitudes affected the crew. Its officers had not, for instance, made sure all the watertight doors and hatches were slammed shut.

At around 1 a.m., these errors were to be among those that cost the lives of 833 men. According to an unnamed survivor mentioned in David Turner's book *Last Dawn*, 'A torpedo from the *U-47* scored a direct hit on the *Royal Oak*'s starboard side, another torpedo started a fire in the magazine, while yet another blew a huge hole in the engine room. Almost immediately, the mighty battleship that had fought in the battle of Jutland keeled over 45 degrees and went to the seabed.'

The informant goes on to describe the chaos that ensued: an inferno raged through the mess-decks with crowds of men racing through flame and fire to leap into the waves of the harbour; in the boiler room, stokers scrambled through clouds of smoke and steam to try and find ladders to allow their escape, only to discover that many of them had been snapped and broken in the overwhelming heat, trapping them below. By this time, the work of the German torpedoes was almost complete. Those who were not killed in the intensity of the initial blaze would meet their end in the chill of the ocean's depths. Some of those who worked on fishing boats and drifters fished them out of the harbour, the fire and oil coating the ocean's surface hindering them in their search. A few searchers were fortunate enough to find the living, but most made the grim discovery of the dead. These included many young boys between the ages of 14 and 18; 137 boys of that age were casualties of the *Royal Oak*. It was this loss that led to the decision shortly afterwards that no one under the age of 18 would be allowed in future to serve on a Royal Navy warship during times of conflict.

There were other ripples from the story, small myths and legends constructed in its wake. Some of these even came from the direction of Berlin where the submarine captain Günther Prien was welcomed home by cheering crowds and an equally cheerful handshake from the Führer, Adolf Hitler. He spoke of how their plans had nearly been foiled by the arrival of a car coming along the road at the water's edge when they surfaced near Graemeshall while making their way out of the confines of Scapa Flow.

'It stopped,' he is quoted as saying in the *News and Journal* of 19 October 1939, 'and the driver got out, apparently to take a good look at us. Then he jumped in the car and drove off at a great pace.'

Clearly his remarks must have generated their own rumours. There had been a dance in the village hall that night and there might have been late-night carousers in the vicinity. People asked each other who the driver of this vehicle might be and why, having seen a submarine making its way out of what, from his description, was clearly Kirk Sound, the individual had not seen fit to report this to the authorities. This was especially the case because the person might have witnessed, too, the blaze of smoke and flame over Kirkwall and would certainly have read the newspapers the following day. What possible reason did they have to remain silent? Clouds of suspicion trailed the rare car-owners of the community with the same steady persistence as the fumes of their exhausts. They must have pointed out in their own defence that, as it was wartime, car headlights were dimmed. They might not have noticed the submarine as they stood outside their vehicles, 'taking the midnight air'.

They were even some who questioned the truth of Prien's words in the paper. Could this be an attempt to mislead the British naval authorities about the true direction the submarine had slipped in and out of the harbour, deliberately trying to point them in the wrong direction in terms of Scapa Flow's flaws and weaknesses? Or was it an attempt to increase his own heroic stature? As if the sheer nerve and daring of Prien's raid wasn't enough, there was the added drama of having carried out his escape under the gaze of some befuddled onlooker who had stumbled upon the scene. Orcadians shook their head as they pondered this, contemplating the smoke and mirrors, the endless questions and suspicions that are always created in the midst of war.

And then there was the paranoia generated in these times. The tale of the Swedish yachtsmen whose boat, the *Thalatta*, sailed 'from Gothenburg to Dublin and back' and was thought to be probing the security of channels leading to the harbour while undertaking that voyage. The story of the young men of the Hitler Youth who were said to have canoed around Scapa Flow, blissfully shouting *'Auf wiedersehen'* to some of the locals standing on an unnamed quayside. There was also the legend of the Kirkwall watchmaker that surfaced as suddenly as the *U-47* on that October night in 1939. In the best traditions of tabloid journalism, he appeared in the US publication the *Saturday Evening Post* in early 1942 under the guise of Alfred Wehring who worked as a Swiss watchmaker in Kirkwall after arriving in Orkney in 1928. His real surname was apparently Oertel and he was seemingly working like clockwork since the beginning of the war, providing information to Dönitz of the U-boat command about the security of Scapa Flow's harbours. It took a denial from the man who would have been his business rival to make clear that Herr Wehring (or Oertel) never existed, and was only a 'journalist's fabrication'.*

Yet even among myths and falsehoods, some truths and certainties emerge. One of these came from the tongue of John Gatt, the skipper of the *Daisy II*, the Fraserburgh boat that had been responsible for the rescue of so many of those who had survived the sinking of the *Royal Oak*. He spoke about the number of foreign trawlers and fishing boats that had sailed into Scapa Flow during both peacetime and the period leading up to World War Two. It would have been an easy matter for them to overhear – or even to discover for themselves – tales of how neglected the defences of the harbour had become, how lack of

---

* This is not to claim that some German espionage did not take place in Orkney. A mapcase with an inscription written in German was discovered in Blanster Farm in South Ronaldsay in 1963. Hidden in a chimney, it appeared to have been made in the Krupps Works in 1917.

care and attention had led to a situation where submarines could easily weave their way through rocks, sandbanks and blockships to let loose a salvo or two at any of His Majesty's ships that were anchored there. And after that, it was simple to wreak havoc. In the words of the Board of Enquiry, 'nothing short of a miracle could have saved the *Royal Oak* after the torpedoes had struck.'

It was inevitable that the roar of the explosion that followed would find its echoes in the streets of Berlin. Hitler's words reminded the crowds there of the scale of Prien's triumph and how it had been 'achieved in the very place where a weak Germany had surrendered its entire fleet in 1918', filling them with a sense that this was finally their nation's hour. The moment was coming when, after the invasion of Norway, Scapa Flow would be under the control of the German fleet and then the people of Britain, too, would soon be looking up at a Nazi flag flapping above their town halls and government buildings. Amidst it all, the young children of Kirkwall left their school-desks to look at a dogfight taking place above the town and young Dorothy cowered as she tried not to see the Luftwaffe drop their bombs a short distance from her home.

The whole country felt a sense of humiliation at the mention of the names 'Scapa Flow' and '*Royal Oak*'. Those words filled the British people with fear and foreboding, knowing that the Germans had breached one of the most secure corners of their citadel and destroyed one of the nation's greatest ships. Such an incident did not augur well for the conflict that was growing and gathering all around them.

It did not augur well at all ...

༚

The people of Germany were not the only nation cheering in the early stages of the war.

There were those in Italy whose voices were loud in triumph when they gathered in Piazza Venezia in Rome on 10 June 1940 for the long-anticipated declaration of war against Britain and France. They met there to see their newly-appointed Supreme Commander of the Forces in the Field, Mussolini, stand upon a balcony and deliver his exhortation to arms to the Italian nation as a whole.

'Fighting men of the land, the sea and the air,' he declared, 'Blackshirts of the Revolution and of the Legions, men and women of Italy, of the Empire and of the Kingdom of Albania, hearken! An hour marked by destiny is striking in the sky of our country; the hour of irrevocable decisions. We are entering the lists against the plutocratic and reactionary democracies of the west...'

He followed this with the argument that it was his country's moral duty to step into the field with Germany, whose military had driven the Allied Forces all the way back to Dunkirk early in May and looked – rather conveniently for Mussolini – as if they were on the very edge of victory. After all, they were also against Britain and France who in so many ways 'had always hindered the advance of the Italian people'. His boulder jaw jutting over those who had assembled before him, his bald head shining, he concluded with a further surge of rhetoric, a rise and fall of words that carried many of those in the piazza with him, their voices loud and cheering, arms raised in powerful Fascist salutes.

'*DUCE! DUCE! DUCE!*'

'Proletarian and Fascist Italy is for the third time on her feet, strong, proud and united as never before,' he continued. 'The single and categorical watchword is binding for us all. Already it is through the air and kindling hearts from the Alps to the Indian Ocean – Conquer...'

Again, there were loud cries as Mussolini's speech roared onward, his strangely high-pitched voice echoing as the people looked up at him, resplendent in his uniform. Many of them were extremely proud of the man and could provide a thousand reasons why they felt this way. He was, after all, one of them. The son of a blacksmith, he had been brought up in a tumbledown farmhouse near Predappio in Romagna in the north of Italy – one that had been adorned with a plaque that emphasised his sense of solidarity with the poor, the fact that he was 'a man of the people'. It read quite simply, 'On this farm Mussolini's peasant ancestors lived and worked.'

He appealed to those Italians who had fought in the First World War by being seen as an 'ordinary soldier' who had served in their ranks. His war diary was one of the more important texts for the regime; his soul, like those of thousands of others who had served in the armed forces, reforged in the fight against the dying empire of Austria–Hungary. There was his physical strength; he was often photographed bare-chested as he worked, perhaps scything through a field of corn or, taking up his father's trade, hammering a horseshoe on an anvil. There was his youth and energy. When Mussolini took up the office of prime minister, he was the youngest the country had ever possessed. His energy could even be seen in the number of mistresses he took to his bed. His wife Rachele knew of the existence of 20 or so, but remained loyal to him. She just shrugged and asked, 'And what of it?'

And then there were other personal qualities. His intellect was prized by those who came into contact with him. Possessing a remarkable memory, he would reel off facts and statistics when foreign visitors or members of his government came before him, asking them – in his usual theatrical manner – to 'forgive my learned references' when he dipped into French or German. For all his undoubted vanity and the brutality of a large number in the movement that he led, he was viewed by many as being kind and compassionate. Speaking to those whose spirits had been broken by the poverty and hunger of the south, he had wept with pity and declared, 'I will care for you. I too have known hunger.'

'*DUCE! DUCE! DUCE!* Believe! Obey! Fight!' they chanted each time they saw him, remembering how before his coming, Italy had been a divided, fractured state, riven by regional and political disputes. A patchwork of different tongues, from Ladin and German in the north to Sard and Sicilian in the islands to the south, it found its unity within Mussolini's strong, muscular form. More than any French monarch who had used the phrase, he was entitled to announce, '*L'état c'est moi . . .*'

In the early years of his government, they could point to some evidence that Il Duce and his mix of personal magic and harsh medicine worked. The long quarrel between Church and State had been finally healed by the concordat he had signed with the Vatican in 1929. He had brought an end to the wave of strikes and political instability that had crippled the country before he came into power. He had balanced national budgets, particularly those of the Post Office and the railway system. To many admirers throughout the world he had, in the words of his fictional Scottish admirer, Miss Jean Brodie, 'performed feats of magnitude' even to the extent that 'unemployment is even farther abolished under him than it was last year'.

Muriel Spark's little joke reveals, however, a greater truth. There was always an aspect of both flash and fakery in Mussolini's triumphs. He trumpeted the creation of railways, the reclamation of marshlands, the building of harbours. However, pointing out both the level of corruption and errors in these constructions, the Italian writer Luigi Barzini argues that the sum total of Fascist achievements 'seem out of proportion to the noise surrounding them, their fame and moral cost'.

This was even more true of the dreams of empire he had given them. The invasion of modern-day Ethiopia (or Abyssinia) may have been viewed as both unpopular and immoral abroad, but it was perceived differently at home where it was seen as a return to the great days when the legions of Imperial Rome marched across North Africa and Asia Minor. There was, too, the bloody-handed way he had tightened his country's hold over Albania and Libya, the support he had given to Franco and his Falangist forces in Spain.

And now there was this moment, the hour when he stood upon the balcony in Rome, justifying his decision to enter the war on Germany's side. Listening to the crowd shout '*DUCE! DUCE! DUCE!*', it was easy to convince himself they believed implicitly in the slogan that was painted on thousands of walls throughout Italy: '*Mussolini ha sempre ragione.* Mussolini is always right.' There was no sign of any questions, no evidence of doubt.

'We will conquer,' he promised as their cries resounded, 'and we will give finally a long period of peace with justice to Italy, to Europe and to the world. People of Italy, to arms! Show your tenacity and your worth.'

Yet the truth was that some among the 2 million or so members of the Fascist party wondered whether on this occasion their leader was right. They had doubts about their ally, one that had so recently and ruthlessly vanquished their fellow Catholics in Poland. They had questions about how ready their armed forces were to fight in any long and sustained war. Their tanks had been chosen for economic reasons. Far cheaper than heavier models, their single virtue was that he could have more of them at lower costs. They were small and tinny, and easily pierced by machinegun fire. The armoured divisions were sometimes forced to borrow vehicles from the police to use in a military parade. The navy had neither a fleet air arm nor an aircraft carrier. It even lacked radar, never, according to Barzini, possessing even the slightest suspicion that 'such an invention existed'.

And among the sceptics was, in fact, the man who stepped from the balcony that evening, hearing the roars and cheers below. His whole performance had been a triumph of theatricality over uncertainty. Mussolini was all too aware that his country's armed forces were not remotely ready for war. A number of his generals had told him how weak they were: instead of the great numbers they trumpeted, there were only ten divisions among the front-line troops; there were no real anti-aircraft defences; and far from benefiting the country, some of Il Duce's imperial adventures had damaged it, both economically and militarily . . .

Such things did not augur well for the conflict that was growing and gathering all around him.

They did not augur well at all . . .

༃

Let us move from one leader to another – one who like Mussolini can stir a crowd with his words, move them on a wave of rhetoric with high-blown phrases and the gestures of his arms. He stands this time not on a balcony overlooking a city square but on a quay in Kirkwall, looking out, perhaps, on a stretch of water not far from Scapa Flow, a place that has known too many deaths and bloodshed – from the days of Olaf Tryggvason and Earl Sigurd of Orkney, Haakon Haakonsson of Norway returning from the Battle of Largs in 1263, and the invasions from Caithness in 1529. So many corpses lying undisturbed for centuries among the silt and rock, sand and seaweed. It would be impossible to count them all. And now with this latest disaster, the sailors of the *Royal Oak*. The murk and swirl of the waters that stretch wide before him conceal the bodies of men lying broken and twisted countless fathoms below.

He looks around the harbour, speaking urgently and with authority. As he waves an arm, his fingers are not arranged in his trademark 'V for Victory' sign. Instead, he stubs his forefinger in what he imagines is the direction of the bay's eastern defences, asking the question that had come earlier to his lips while bending over an Admirality chart in London: 'These must be closed! How long will it take?'

His advisers cough and stumble, wondering how to answer his question. One looks agitated, wondering if all the humiliations of the past few weeks have affected the First Lord of the Admiralty's mind. They know that he has felt them keenly, the fact that the country has lost so many brave men and one of the navy's legendary ships. ('Poor fellows, poor fellows,' he had declared when he was informed, 'trapped in these black depths.') They sense, too, that he is all too aware of how news of this loss will echo through the streets of Berlin, giving their enemy greater hope and confidence, a sign of victory to come. Like him, they are aware of how the sinking was followed a few days later by an air raid that almost sank Admiral Jellicoe's old flagship *Iron Duke* – a vessel that was only saved when tugs from Lyness hauled it into shallow water. There was also another air attack that severely damaged Rosyth, the other anchorage for the Home Fleet on the east side of Scotland, forcing the navy to move its ships to the country's other shoreline, Loch Ewe and the Clyde, far away from combat, Germans and the continent of Europe, too near to the city of Glasgow which, according to Churchill, is full of Irish traitors.

'These must be closed! How long will it take?'

The question echoes, takes on reverberations from other events. This man, Winston Churchill, had visited Orkney the previous September and, noting the poorly-defended anchorage, had demanded there should be more blockships and nets. In his possession at that time had been a locked box of papers which he had studied as he took the train from London to Wick, papers which detailed the neglected state of the harbour. He had been forced to stand in the House of Commons three days after the sinking, praising the 'remarkable exploit of professional skill and daring' of the U-boat crew whose actions led to the tragedy. Some are all too conscious that if this had happened a month or two later, when the First Lord of the Admiralty had been longer ensconced in his present post, Churchill's political career would be over. Some sense the injustice of the findings of the Admiralty Board of Enquiry which occurred a short time after the torpedoes struck. The board had condemned Scapa Flow's defences, censuring Sir Wilfred French, Admiral Commanding Orkney and Shetland, for their unprepared state. This was despite the fact that he had warned the previous summer of the harbour's failings, going to the extent of volunteering to bring a small ship or submarine himself past the blockships to prove his point.

'These must be closed! How long will it take?' the question echoes.

Answering it is impossible. They know how green water surges sometimes between the Mainland of Orkney and Lamb Holm, Glimps Holm, Burray and that last island, South Ronaldsay. They are aware of how strong the tide can be as it channels through the Sounds – Kirk Sound, Skerry Sound, East Weddel Sound, Water Sound . . . They have seen it stir the hulls of some of the blockships – like the *Seriano* and the *Thames* – chained and harnessed within these channels, the latter with the metal of its hull as thin as a sixpence. The tide plucks up and plays with rocks which man and all the machines at his command would strain and buckle under if they were forced to haul or carry. With its white and toppling crests, there are times when it appears to have the solidity of walls tumbling into the more sheltered waters of the Flow.

And now there is this pompous fool of a politician with his absurd and persistent question. 'These must be closed. How long will it take?'

They might be tempted to reply that this would depend on the magical forces they were able to call upon, for it seems to them that it would be real wizardry to transform this stretch of ever-shifting water to firm, dependable land. They might do this – but they know that Churchill has already been charged to perform the impossible. Each day's headlines give them a sense of the scale of the task both he – and they – have before them. There are endless omens and auguries in the news as the conflict grows and gathers all around them. They do not envy his task of steeling men for the battle that lies ahead.

So instead, others try to answer him. By his side, there are men like Sir Arthur Whittaker who has accompanied Churchill on his journey north. He probably unfolded a chart of the eastern approaches to Scapa Flow, his hand pointing out the locations of

Lamb Holm, Glimps Holm, Burray, South Ronaldsay, and the channels of water that lie between them. The First Lord might have chomped at his cigar while he listened to these explanations. Impatient with the detail, he was likely to have decided already that barriers could and should be built between these islands. He only wished to know the answer to the question he had asked before. 'How long will it take?'

Those who answer probably seek to baffle him with science, the kind of rational answers always provided by practical men of good sense. They speak of the hydrographic surveys that are required of the various Sounds; how experiments are required to see if any materials dumped into their currents will either lie there or be swept away; whether the geological department of the Ordnance Survey will be able to discover places where good quality rock for this kind of endeavour can be quarried. He probably only half-hears these men speak, listening to them in much the same way as he did when members of his own party spoke in defence of the Munich Agreement, sacrificing Czechoslovakia for a year or so of peace. ('This is only the beginning of the reckoning,' he had predicted. 'This is only the first sip, the first foretaste of a bitter cup . . .') He had already decided what had to be done. It was up to others to ensure that his words turned into truth, that the gap between the insubstantiality of dream and the solidity of stone might be bridged.

༢

There are others who are finding such a distance impossible to cross, who are discovering a chasm exists between a politician's visions and the everyday realities of life and war. Chief among them is Mussolini himself. As the conflict goes on, he becomes slower and heavier; his elephant step ponderous as it echoes through the corridors of his house in Rome or Rocca delle Caminate, the castle in Romagna where he spends much of his time. His hidden uncertainties have begun to have an effect on him. Dark shadows his eyes. He has gained a massive amount of weight. His boulder jaw now jutting outwards above thick rolls of flesh, he fulminates against all whom he believes have crossed him. One day it might be Franco, the Spanish leader for whom he did so much to bring into power. The next it might be his allies, the Germans, and all the times they had betrayed and let him down. Mostly, however, it would be his own people, the Italians – the ones whose loyalty to him for so many years was such that he might have been the puppet-master and they his puppets.

'They are not the descendants of Romans,' he claimed, 'but of foreign slaves, mongrels, serfs.'

As his dreams crumble and fade, Mussolini senses disobedience in his own people, the thought that all they can do is let him down.

Take the average Italian soldier, for instance. When he marched to war for the first time, the words of the Fascist anthem '*Vincere*' ('Winning') were often in his head. Its opening lines are a pastiche of Mussolini's own favourite phrases, each word pounded in his head by the stamping of boots, the clash of arms. They offered him a barricade, strong armour he could shelter and shield himself behind.

> *Temprata da mille passioni*
> *La voce d'Italia squillò:*
> *'Centurie, Coorti, Legioni*
> *In piedi che l'ora suonò!'*

> Steeled by a thousand passions,
> The voice of Italy cried loud:
> 'Centurions, Cohorts, Legions,
> Stand up for the hour has struck!'

The soldiers might have been emboldened for the coming conflict by some of the many slogans that helped to define Mussolini's rule: 'Better to live one day as a lion than a hundred years as a sheep'; 'War is to man what maternity is to a woman'; 'If I advance, follow me! If I retreat, kill me! If I die, avenge me!'

For the less warlike among them, there are also the reassurances that their politicians and generals offer. 'It will not be long before the conflict is over,' they say quietly, echoing the phrases that a previous generation who occupied their ranks whispered before the previous Great War: 'We'll be home by Christmas.' They point to the news headlines as evidence for this view, reasoning that German troops have forced the British to retreat from Dunkirk; that they stand guard, too, on the coastline of Norway a short distance from the islands to the north of Scotland; that, in act of desperation that old warmonger Churchill is now prime minister of Britain . . .

It is men like Primavera and Micheloni, electricians by trade, who console themselves with this thought, believing it will not be long before they return to their former line of work. Buttapasta, a cement worker, trusts the same will happen, preferring the building site to the battleground. And those of strong faith utter prayers to whatever saint their lives are sheltered under, believing that in these words there is the possibility of a swift end to the conflict. Domenico Chiocchetti taps the tiny picture of the Madonna and Child contained in his breast pocket, crossing himself as he does this. Given to him by his mother, it is based upon the painting *Madonna of the Olives* by Nicolò Barabino. Wearing a white shawl, the haloed likeness of the Blessed Virgin holds the Infant Jesus in her arms, looking down at the way he stretches out an olive branch in his hand. Domenico is a peaceful-minded man; he hopes and prays that one day mankind will reach out and grasp the olive branch from Christ's fingers. For all Domenico's love of his new nation, Italy, of which his province of Trentino-Alto Adige in the north of that country only became part after the Great War, he does not feel comfortable clutching a rifle, not – as Mussolini in his palace in Romagna knows only too well – that it is much of a rifle.

Like most of the other soldiers, Chiocchetti, Primavera and Micheloni must have been all too conscious of the inadequacy of much of the equipment they had been provided for the fight. No doubt some of the soldiers moaned about its shortcomings with the same persistence as a talking cricket whispered in Pinocchio's ear about the direction in which he was taking his life. ('If you think these will do, my friend, you must have a wooden head.') Some of their rifles were antiquated museum-pieces out of date for the purposes of modern warfare. The tanks employed in their armoured divisions were poorly designed, underpowered and undergunned. Only a small part of their forces, especially in North Africa, was motorised. For much of the conflict that took place there, unmotorised infantry was forced to play a major role.*

And then there were the Italian officers. Men like De Vitto, Fornasier and Pennisi must have seen the differences between them and their German counterparts when the two forces met in the North African desert. The officers of Rommel's forces ate the same rations as the rest of the men. They suffered the same living conditions. Not so the ones the Italian troops observed. Apart from a few divisions such as the Italian paratroops, the Folgore, they were part of the country's aristocratic elite and owed a great deal more loyalty to their king, Victor Emmanuel III, than they did to the Fascist movement. They enjoyed comparative luxury as their forces moved across the North African desert. They behaved somewhat like the lions praised and extolled in Mussolini's slogans, eating the greater share of the allotted rations while the unpromoted men looked on. Their hunger – like their sense of frustration – kept growing with every day they spent in the desert, fighting the British and Australian troops. Like him, they must have spent much of their time regretting that they had ever left their homes.

---

* There were exceptions to this. The Italian machine gun and Breda aircraft were highly valued. What little motor transport existed was also of good quality.

It was not the only way their officers let them down. The ordinary soldiers were largely a peasant army; many of them only had the most basic schooling. They knew little about the strange new environment in which they found themselves and were forced to contend with the chilly nights, the weather that alternated between a scourging, dry heat or heavy rain. There were the flies, too, clustering in thick clouds above the empty, bare terrain. Having only the most basic knowledge of hygiene, the Italian trenches and dug-outs were also plagued by lice. Their light tropical shirts and tunics – known as the *Sahariana* – were infested by the tiny creatures; their bites and scratches often irritated by sand blown into each tiny cut by the force of the *khamsin*, the constant desert wind. And through all this chafing and itching, their officers just looked on, never offering them any help or advice on how to deal with the conditions they found in the desert.

In this, they were just like their predecessors in the Great War: badly led. They had neither the means nor the opportunity to take on their opponents on equal terms. The Allied Forces also sought to humiliate them on every occasion, trying to divide the Italian soldiers from the German forces they fought alongside. In the press and propaganda broadcast by the Allies, the Italians were portrayed as weak and cowardly, racing away from the battle at the earliest possible opportunity. Rather than take them prisoners, the Australian forces, for instance, were known to send them back to their own side with the seat cut out of their trousers.

Humiliation seeps into the soul. Scorn can bite as sharp as bullets. It had its basis in battles like Sidi Barrani and Beda Fomm where the Italians surrendered in vast numbers. In the former, a short time after a brief and half-hearted battle, one British soldier reported that when he looked out at the township 'it was like washday out there; whites were showing everywhere, and the Italians were climbing on each other's shoulders to show white flags.'

And when they were captured, many 'made it quite clear that they did not want any part of this war and made derogatory remarks about Mussolini, their great leader. They were very happy and relieved to be prisoners.'

Like the man in his castle in Romagna, the Italian soldiers, too, must have fulminated against all those who had let them down and betrayed them: those Fascist politicians and generals who had told them that the conflict would be over by Christmas. They thought of the fox and the cat in the book they had read as children, trying to deceive Pinocchio into planting his few gold coins in the Field of Miracles in the hope of reaping a harvest of thousands. The soldiers now saw their masters as men with wide mouths and long noses, leading them to their own Field of Miracles, telling ordinary Italians extraordinary lies.

And then there were those who took refuge in familiar, more long-lasting truths. They thanked St George for protecting them in warfare, trusted themselves now to the shelter of St Leonard as they rose to their feet under the gaze of the forces they had opposed. They thought of their families at home, their likenesses captured in faded pictures, smiling benignly at their husbands, fathers, lovers, sons. They prayed, too, to the Blessed Virgin whose image was portrayed on the card placed within the top pocket of their tunics, hoping that one day men would snatch the olive branch from the fingers of the Child she carried, allowing those whose necks chafed against the collars of their uniforms to return home and find peace . . .

3

STUMBLING STONES

AND ON THIS ROCK

And so we bring whatever layer of stone
on which we took our first steps
to this solitary location - igneous, sedimentary, metamorphic,
and honour them as our foundations
whether these be granite, slate or chalk,
Orcadian sandstone, marble, quartz.
This is what kept faith with us,
permitting us to walk upon whatever edge of earth
to which our early lives belonged,
allowing soles to hold sway over water,
stay firm before wind's onslaught, the awesome weight of salt.
It, too, provides these walls for us,
barriers behind which we can whisper, say our prayers,
giving ground where we can kneel or stand tall,
granting us an echo when we tell our petty troubles
to the peace and hush of air.

'This is what it looked like first of all,' he says.

John Muir guides me to a door concealed by a gold curtain

at the far end of the Chapel. A quick turn of a Yale key and the secrets of the building are revealed. There is corrugated iron at this hidden section of the Nissen hut on the island of Lamb Holm at the southern end of Orkney, covered only by a coat of yellow paint. One can see what it must have looked like before the transformation occurred – an anonymous, barely serviceable place before Domenico Chiocchetti and his fellow Italian prisoners of war got to work on it, performing a metamorphosis similar to that of a carpenter hewing and giving shape to a wooden log, carving it to perfection. Before the arrival of the prisoners, the walls were dull, anonymous and mute; now, in the main part of the hut, they speak of brightness, life and faith.

There are chairs folded on the floor, the boxes that line one side sealed and fastened tight by a printed tape with the words 'The Orcadian' scrolled across them. They contain hundreds of copies of the booklet, *Orkney's Italian Chapel* for distribution at £1 per copy to this year's crop of tourists. 'There are one or two changes this year,' John explains in his soft Orkney lilt, 'A few more colour pictures. A few misspellings corrected . . .' It is only a small display of mementoes connected with the Chapel that save this part of the building from complete anonymity, from being just one of the many Nissen huts that stand mouldering around the coastline of the north of Scotland. There are a small number of brass plaques gifted by individuals and groups in Italy; an Italian flag with a garish feathered cockerel and the letters 'POW' and names like 'Vittorio, Assunto, Ligo . . .' scrawled across it; and, most intriguingly of all, a picture of St Anne in blue and brown, painted on the surface of a hessian turnip sack by an Italian prisoner who was housed in a camp near Fraserburgh on the Scottish mainland. It offers a reminder that Orkney was not the only place in the United Kingdom where Italian servicemen were held captive. They were found too in other parts of Scotland, England and Wales.

'That looks good,' I smile, pointing in its direction. 'Did you ever think of putting it on display?'

'We talked about it once,' John nods, 'but we took a decision to leave the Chapel the way it was. We've added nothing to it.'

I nod, understanding the reasons for this view. It is yet more evidence of the love and affection for this building that John and others like him have demonstrated for many years, the reason why they serve as members of the Chapel Preservation Committee. Stepping back into the main part of the building, I am reminded once again of the reasons why someone might feel this way. There is no doubt of the passion people feel for this place. It is even present in John's hushed voice, the quiet way this grey-haired man steps through the building, gesturing towards the illustrations colouring its walls, the skill seen in its ironwork, the holy water stoup crafted from cement.

The Chapel might even have played some miracles in John's own life, widening his horizons. When we enjoy a cup of tea in his house later, his blue eyes shine brightly when he speaks about going to Yosemite National Park in California, founded by one of America's greatest and most well-known Scotsmen, his namesake, John Muir from Dunbar in East Lothian. When the receptionist discovered both his name and nationality, she took out the visitors' book, opening it to a fresh page. 'You're going to have this one all on your own. No one else is going to write on it.'

We talk briefly about an incident in the life of John Muir the naturalist – an industrial accident temporarily blinded him and made him determined, when he recovered, to enjoy what remained of his days. He resolved not to spend any longer working within a factory's walls but instead to rejoice in the shade of California's sequoia trees and the wonders of the new continent his existence had chanced upon. There is something of that in the Orcadian John Muir too. His life has been transformed by the coincidence of being born and brought up on the opposite side of Kirk Sound from the Italian Chapel. It provided both him – and the entire community – with its own awakening, its own miraculous change in the way they viewed the world.

There is evidence of this awakening just before the turn from the Orkney mainland that leads to the Chapel. Rather oddly on this treeless isle, a carved totem pole stands a short distance away from the end of the first Barrier. It was transplanted there a number of years ago, the shared work of native Orcadians that came from the vicinity of Holm and people from the Squamish First Nation who came from the opposite edge of the world. With its runic inscription, its crab, seals and puffin, its presence acts as a reminder that islandmen had relationships with Cree women when they were employed by the Hudson's Bay Company in the northern extremes of Canada in the eighteenth and nineteenth century. Over the last few years, descendants of the offspring of these unions have come back to Orkney, picking up once again family ties that had for years been loose or lost.

And then there is the road that takes my car from John's home to the Chapel. For the people of, say, South Ronaldsay, this road, more than anything else, transformed their relationship with the outside world. It speeds across the concrete of the Churchill Barriers, crossing the four islands and their various Sounds, making it possible for residents to work in the shops and offices of Kirkwall, and to catch a flight to Glasgow, Inverness or Edinburgh from the airport on the edge of that town. Apart from a few exceptionally stormy days in the year when the Barriers are closed to road traffic, residents can visit relatives or attend appointments at the Balfour Hospital. They have become both part and parcel of the whole. No longer are these islands on their own, divided from each other and the Orkney mainland by a barricade of salt and tide.

The geography of Orkney makes these connections more vital than they would be on the mainland areas of Scotland. Orkney comprises a scattering of some 70 islands, all grouped around the one known as the Mainland with its capital, Kirkwall. Only 21 of these are inhabited. To the north of the Mainland, there are islands with exotic names like Shapinsay, Rousay, Egilsay,

Wyre, Westray, Eday, Sanday, Stronsay, Papa Westray and North Ronaldsay. Veer south and the visitor will find Hoy, Graemsay and Flotta. There exists a delicate web of transport links and connections to take a person from place to place. You can touch down on an aircraft and land on Westray, Papa Westray, North Ronaldsay. On Hoy, Graemsay, Flotta, you are limited to arriving by ferry, often crossing bitter, storm-ravaged seas in winter. In the case of Burray, Lamb Holm, Glimps Holm and South Ronaldsay, a car, grocery van or even the luxury of a Massey Ferguson tractor can take a person or the proverbial little pig all the way home from the supermarket.

Despite this, the Barriers were not designed primarily for the convenience of commuters. Like their counterpart in the Outer Hebrides which runs between Benbecula and South Uist, their existence is due to a military presence in the area. They came into being as a result of Churchill's desire to answer an urgent enquiry. It was one he repeated over and over during the months when they were first being constructed, thinking continually of the safety of the Royal Navy ships anchored in the Flow.

'These must be closed! How long will it take?'

Churchill knew that if there was to be any possibility of Britain winning the war, this task had to be completed as quickly as possible.

There was another thought, however, that motivated Churchill, one that stirs many politicians almost as much as their love for their own country. He saw the possibility of another sinking as a threat to the survival of his own recently resurrected political career. Brooding on his previous experience of office during the First World War, he knew only too well how First Lords of the Admiralty were treated when great ships were sunk or things went wrong. They became victims of both the envious and ambitious among the parliamentary ranks. He revealed his fears in his personal correspondence: 'They will hang us all if it happens again.'

His anxiety generated an avalanche of 'Action This Day' minutes: a series of demands for plain and simple answers to difficult and complex questions. 'How much has been done now? Are we making progress?' Subordinates must have quaked at both the impatience and insistence with which he asked them. Each of his demands and enquiries had the same power and force as the waves that surged through Kirk Sound, a similar persistence to the seas that passed between Burray and South Ronaldsay; they rose and fell with the regularity and strength of the tide. They would have felt that they were being asked to undertake an act of alchemy, changing water into land for this bald, old man striding through the corridors of all the offices of power in the nation's distant capital.

Success in this transformation depended on men of business and men of science. Only a combination of these two kinds of people could ensure the transformation would occur.

The men of science were called upon first. They were deployed in order for the First Lord of the Admiralty to obtain a response to his enquiry – whether the magic of transforming narrow sea-channels into thin stretches of land could be performed. The various Sounds were plumbed and charted by the survey ship, *Franklin*. On occasions, it was not the only vessel out checking the lie of both land and water for this purpose. Fishing boats were commandeered and used beside this boat. An occasional rowing boat was seen bobbing up and down nearby, an engineer at their oars while another took notes and measurements. These vessels checked the tides, currents and waves prevalent in the area, noting each rock, reef and sandbank that existed both above and below its waterline. An academic from Leeds University, Professor Gibson, used this information as the basis for a series of experiments as to whether the materials deposited there would stay in place or be carried away by the surge of the sea. Noting each relevant measurement, he came to the conclusion that the conjuring trick Churchill had demanded of them could be done.

It is at this point that the men of business became involved, helping the scientists in their work. The well-known firm Balfour Beatty was informed of Mr Churchill's strange ambition, and began negotiations to buy four cableways in order to make sure his plans became a reality. They were joined soon by Messrs John Henderson Ltd who were asked to help adapt the cableways, employing their strength in the same way that they were used in the building of a barrage across the river Tigris in a place called Kut-El-Amara in Iraq. Clearly the conditions in that dry, dusty part of the world were very different from those in Orkney; the swirl of wind and sea very different from those within a desert kingdom. This is a place where the powerful currents of the North Sea and the Atlantic Ocean meet in the Pentland Firth. The civil engineer in chief, Sir Arthur Whittaker, had already noted that 'the fast-flowing tide would bank up as much as forty feet higher on one side of a blockship than on the other, and cascade over her semi-submerged deck like a waterfall.'

The resident superintending civil engineer in charge of the project, C. Gordon Nicol, put these difficulties in a more poetic context. In his notes used to accompany lectures about the project, he wrote of how 'at the time of high water spring tides, the roar of the currents, boiling round, under and sometimes over the blockships was like that of a mighty waterfall and on a sunny day the colours merge from deepest purple to palest green with pure white spray leaping in the air'.

Adding to the 'hubble, bubble, toil and trouble' of the tidal race, which was bound to increase in intensity as work progressed and the channel narrowed, were the frequent high winds that affect an island location. Another academic, Professor Jack Allen of Aberdeen University, was called upon to consider how they could drop huge and heavy burdens from the cables without putting into danger the ropeways below. He factored the strength of the wind into his calculations, probably noting with dismay the force and fury of the storms that so often afflicted the islands.

It was a storm, for instance, that led to the sinking of the drifter *Token*; it was swept up by waves and became stuck on some rocks in Skerry Sound during the creation of the Barriers.

Yet there were hidden advantages within Orkney's borders. One of these was the rock to be found there, the geological department of the Ordnance Survey having identified areas where suitable material could be excavated and used. One of the most convenient sites was Moss Quarry in Holm, a short distance away, close enough for old lorries to roll up and down the road between the two places, extending the stretch of road they travelled yard by slow yard. Others were in Burray, Lamb Holm, Tankerness, elsewhere in Orkney. It was not, however, a simple task to obtain this stone. It had to be hewed, hacked and hauled out of the land. Explosives were employed to do this, placed like tiny candles within each line or flaw found within the rock, the expertise of men from Ballachulish in Argyll employed to assist them in this task. Excavators were needed too. Purchased throughout the whole length of the United Kingdom and even the United States, they had to be brought to Orkney, taken across the sea to the island's shores. Even when that was done, the work was not complete. There had to be diesel to fuel them. And, too, there were pumps, scrapers, a drilling plant – all of which needed vast quantities of electric power. For these, generators had to be provided. This required the creation of large electric generators, sheltered in buildings which needed strong foundations and walls, protecting them from the whip of wind and weather.

The stone that they were quarrying was only the foundation of the Barriers between the islands. Huge concrete slabs were placed on top, then lowered into position by Blondins, a pulley system named after the French tightrope walker and designed to carry large burdens over chasms or channels of water. Ten miles of track are needed, 58 locomotives with 260 wagons attached, 2 tug ships, 24 cranes, 16 crushers, 19 excavators, 12 dumper trucks, 51 lorries, and accommodation for the hundreds of men who will be employed there. The last might take the form of large accommodation ships and a temporary village of Nissen huts on the ground, complete with cookhouses and toilets.

Among all the different voices, those labouring and those whose organisation and planning ensures that stores and equipment are brought to the shores of Orkney, there is one that is more insistent than any other. Churchill asks a tumult of questions. They range from the availability of duffel coats for those on winter duty on destroyers to the 'rest and recreation facilities' available for servicemen on Orkney. Above all, he tries to ascertain how the transformation of the fleet's defences at Scapa Flow have been progressing, and how much work has been done since his orders – known as 'Plan R' – were issued.

' . . . How many blockships (have been) sunk? How many nets made? How many men have been in work for how many days? What buildings have been erected? What gun sites have been concreted and prepared? What progress has been made? . . .'

In a minute sent to Admiral Pound, the First Sea Lord, he fires another question, one which shows both his frustration and alarm: 'The Navy demands Scapa and Rosyth both to be kept at its highest point. Do you realise that perhaps we are heading for *defeat*?'

The urgency in all these questions booms and reverberates, travelling all the way from the corridors of Admiralty House to Orkney and beyond. It plays its part in galvanising those below him, ensuring that miracles might begin to be done.

One of the men who witnessed the miracles lived with his wife at the edge of Lerwick in Shetland. In his mid-eighties, Jim Nicolson was a small, broadly-built man, his thin grey hair swept back on his head, his movements slow and deliberate. He stood up to greet me when I entered, surrounded by the flowers that are among the chief interests of his wife, Pearl. They shade and colour the room, even during the colder seasons of the year – a tribute to the time she spends in the conservatory at the back of the house, preparing plants and cuttings to catch Shetland's rare gleams of sunlight during early spring.

Yet even more than flowers, the couple's deep Christian faith pervaded their home. A picture of praying hands, as careworn as Jim's own, hangs on one wall; a calendar proclaiming the work of a Christian charity is pinned up on another. Beside his chair, there is a collection of books, including the Bible, ready to hand. A number of these betrayed his interest in the place where he once lived. During our conversation, he took out a couple of books about Scapa Flow and the sinking of the *Royal Oak* and passes them over to me. Like Archie Wylie, he talked about the days when Orkney was a dangerous place to be.

'There were no less than four main airports in Orkney during the war years,' he noted, naming them, 'Twatt and Hatston. They were run by the Royal Navy. The Fleet Air Arm, as it was then called. Skaebrae and Grimsetter. These were the two run by the Royal Air Force.' He stopped for a moment to clarify matters. 'Grimsetter, you'll know. That's where Kirkwall airport is today. All around the islands too, there were barrage balloons. Some were attached to positions on the land. Others were out in the North Sea, attached by balloon winches to around 20 fishing trawlers set about the place. All that gives you an idea of how important Orkney was to the war effort at that time.'

The son of a boat-builder who was originally from Shetland, Jim's family had only arrived in Orkney a few years before the war started, coming to St Mary's in 1937. It was, Jim conceded, not the most successful idea his father had ever come up with. 'He didn't realise that the two places had very different ideas about boats. In Shetland, the men are fishermen who sometimes work on the land. In Orkney, it's the other way about.'

Mistaken though the older man's business ideas might have been, it did not take long for the younger one to find work. In an age that did not believe in indulging its offspring, he began with the local firm, Alfie Flett, employed as a joiner for two years from the age of 15. He spent much of his time working with the Admiralty and at the Hatston base.

That changed in 1939 when he went to work for Balfour Beatty. It was, he explains, a way of avoiding call-up for a few years. Being employed on the Barriers meant he was part of a reserved occupation, safe from the perils of a berth in the merchant navy which many men from Scotland's offshore islands had been forced to occupy. In order to do this, he had gone first to the labour exchange in Kirkwall. It was this institution that had sent a large number of men, often Irish labourers, from across the country up to work on the Barriers. Their term of duty was normally three months long, and then they would be employed farther south, desperate to escape – what they saw as – the deprivations of Orkney life. Nevertheless, despite their protests, many stayed on.

'There was one fellow,' Jim recalled, 'who was complaining about the place from the moment I met him, shortly after he was sent there. For all his moaning, he was still there at the end of the war, still talking, too, about leaving.'

Jim was less reluctant to stay. This was his new home, a place where both he and his family had only recently settled. When his visit to the labour exchange failed to bring the result he wanted, he went to speak to Mr Hill, the foreman who was in charge of the work on site. '"Leave it to me," Mr Hill said, and it wasn't long before I was taken on. He had a lot more authority than the labour exchange in Kirkwall . . .'

From there, it was a new existence for the young Jim, moving within and working in the noise and hurly-burly of the new construction site. It was a place which, as a native of St Mary's, he was to some degree familiar with, even conscious of the creation of the Barriers before he was employed to work there. He saw the building of the piers as they are outlined in Alastair and Anne Cormack's excellent book, *Bolsters Blocks Barriers*. Clearly they were a priority – providing the means of landing both equipment and stores at the site. It was the very lack of either of these that hampered the creation of the Barriers initially, forcing them to be 'built in much the same way as piers had been built a hundred years before'. It was a long, slow process that provoked both prayers and swears. Men levered rock from the nearby foreshore, hauling each slab into place, wrestling mounds of stone and laying them down as if every part formed a section of a giant superhuman jigsaw. Slowly but surely, a structure was formed, one that was sturdy enough to bear the weight of a crane or a railway engine. The largest of these poked some 250 feet by 20 feet out into the sea, 'giving twenty feet of water' at the outer end. And with its creation, a miracle was starting to take shape; a sea-channel was being transformed into land, the dreams of engineers and scientists beginning to find some foundation in reality. *

In his new job with Balfour Beatty, young Jim Nicolson was no longer just an observer of all this. Tools in hand, he was at the centre of all the turmoil, helping to create buildings that would serve as a camp for the men who laboured there. He learned how to fashion joints, ensuring doors were perfectly in place and roof beams pitched in the correct position. There were men around him who were good tradesmen, people he could learn from.

An inheritor of his father's care and craft, there were moments when he was dismayed at what he saw going on. 'Some of the wood we got for the huts wasn't exactly the best in terms of quality. Much of it was full of sap. It came up in the mortise holes when you nailed it. And then there was all that lovely, good wood thrown down and used for dumper ramps – six by twelve – an awful waste it was. An awful waste.' He shook his head sadly as he thought of this. 'But I don't suppose it was anyone's fault that was happening. The whole thing had to be done quickly.'

There was little doubt about that. Recent events had contrived to increase the urgency of the task. By May 1940, Norway had

---

* There were, however, continual problems. The red stone from the Glimps Holm quarry disintegrated in salt water. The narrowing of the channel increased the power and surge of water passing through the remaining gap.

fallen; German troops were now stationed a short distance away from the shoreline of Holm, where young Dorothy Rendall walked and played. The politician who had harried men like Sir Arthur Whittaker and Admiral Pound was now in Downing Street, having become prime minister in the aftermath of that event. Ears straining to listen to their crystal sets in June 1940, they heard that familiar accent with its slow and exact delivery, uttering words that have become long familiar to us.

'We shall defend our island whatever the cost may be; we shall fight on the beaches; we shall fight on the landing grounds; we shall fight in the fields and the streets; we shall fight in the hills; we shall never surrender.'

They looked down once more at what had been constructed of the Barriers, built to defend the waters of the Orkney Islands, and heard once again the echo of the questions they had heard from Churchill's lips when he was still First Lord of the Admiralty: 'What buildings have been erected? What gun sites have been concreted and prepared? What progress has been made...?

'How long will it take...?'

༈

Even the Italians imprisoned in Egypt were becoming familiar with Churchill's words – that strange, drawn-out accent, that peculiar and contemptuous way he pronounced the single word 'Nnnaaazzziiisss' droning round their heads in much the same irritable way as the thousands of desert flies that plagued and tormented them. They tried not to listen when he spoke to them – that deep and sonorous voice condemning the fact that Britain and Italy were at war with one another, each committed to the 'other's ruin'. Even as early into his premiership as 23 December 1940, a few short days before Christmas, he addressed the Italian population, knowing that the majority of his audience shook their heads at his suggestion that the sole cause of the conflict was 'one man, and one man alone: Mussolini', and did all they could to ignore the fact that the British prime minister was quoting both from his and the Italian leader's letters to back up his claims. It was all propaganda, wasn't it? All British lies and falsehoods. What else could they expect from an old British warmonger like him?

Still the old man's words kept returning to their ears, permeating their hearing no matter how much they tried to bat, flap or wave his message away. For all that they tried to ignore him, they couldn't help hearing him praise Mussolini as 'a great man', but also criticise the 'horrid verge of ruin' to which he had led his country. 'Anyone can see who it was wanted peace, and who it was that meant to have war. One man and one man only was resolved to plunge Italy after all these years and strain and effort into the whirlpool of war.'

Comparing their new ally Adolf Hitler to Attila the Hun, he spoke of the German forces, referring to the Führer's 'hordes of ravenous soldiery and [his] gangs of Gestapo policemen'. In words thick with irony, Churchill told the prisoners that it was German forces that now occupied, held down and protected 'the Italian people, for whom [Hitler] and his Nazi followers cherish the most bitter and outspoken contempt that is on record between races'. Coming to a tremulous conclusion, he incited their nation to rise up against the man who had strutted before them in Piazza Venezia in Rome some six months before, declaring 'an hour marked by destiny' had arrived. Contrasting this with the grim reality of war, he informed them, 'this is where one man, and one man only, has led you: and there I leave this unfolding story until the day comes – as come it will – when the Italian nation will once more take a hand in shaping its own fortunes.'

His words, and many others like them, hung in the air of the prison camp in Geneifa, provoking a range of different reactions in the men who heard them. There were some who responded to the situation with a simple catchphrase, one that they would repeat to any British person who came within earshot of them until Capitulation Day when Italy finally surrendered to the inevitable and went over to the Allied side. They said this whether they agreed with it or not, knowing the words were expected to be on their lips. 'Mussolini – very good man. Churchill – very bad man . . .'

There were those, too, who had learned to treat the words of all politicians with the same cynicism as they had regarded the false promises of the cat and the fox when they tried to trick Pinocchio in the pages of their childhood story. 'Someone else trying to make us believe in a Field of Miracles . . . These types of men are all the same . . .'

And there were others whose cynicism ran even deeper, privately agreeing with all the British leader said. They had never been that convinced by Mussolini's boasts of a 'new Roman Empire', knowing in their hearts that their country's military strength did not match their leader's bombast. They knew that he had entered the war reluctantly that evening on the Piazza Venezia, doing so at the behest of Hitler or, as the *New York Times* succinctly put it, with all 'the courage of a jackal at the heels of a bolder beast of prey'. As a result of this, for all his pretences, he was far from being the puppet-master but simply the marionette. Instead of recreating the glory that was Rome, they felt it was more likely that he was laying down the foundation stones for German dreams of a Thousand Year Reich or, as Churchill put it in April 1941, 'a vassal state of Hitler's Empire.'

There was, after all, a profound distrust between the two people, one that was bred deep within their bones.* Some of the older ones had seen German guns turned against them, their artillery aimed in their direction in battles like Caporetto in the upper Isonzo valley in the north of Italy. Occurring in the last

---

* One of the former prisoners refers to this when interviewed on his return to Orkney.

week of October 1917, it was a time when German forces, fighting alongside the crumbling, hated Austro-Hungarian Empire, almost defeated the Italian army and did so with a combination of breathtaking skill and meticulous military planning. Mark Thompson's powerful and authoritative book *The White War* sums up the results of a time that was seen as a national disgrace and humiliation in a single paragraph, the grim total of a few short days of bloodshed that almost turned the outcome of the First World War completely around.

> The statistics of defeat were dizzying. The Italians lost nearly 12,000 dead, 30,000 wounded and 294,000 prisoners. In addition, there were 350,000 disbanded men, roaming around or making for home. Only half of the army's sixty-five divisions survived intact, and half the artillery had been lost: more than 3,000 guns, as well as 300,000 rifles, 3,000 machine guns, 1,600 motor vehicles and so forth. Territorially, some 14,000 square kilometres were lost, with a population of 1,150,000 people.

The younger men may have heard from the lips of their fathers some other details of that battle, the result of which was reversed a short time later with the help of Allied troops. These perhaps included stories of the sheer destruction caused by the barrage of artillery shells let loose that day, the heaviest fired on the Italian Front during the conflict. There were tales, too, of the effects of the poison gas mingling with the fog cloaking their positions that morning, created from a mixture of diphenylchloroarsine and phosgene. Their masks were powerless to protect those who wore them – they were designed for chlorine gas rather than the equally deadly fare that surrounded them. Some 700 men were found stiff and frozen in their positions after the arrival of that thick, yellow mist.

Yet there are other, more recent reasons for the distrust between the two people. The Italian prisoners had long ago come to resent the way the German soldiers regarded them. They imagined clicks of disapproval in their voices every time they gathered to speak that harsh, unfathomable tongue of theirs, condemning the chaos brought upon them by their partners in their pact of steel. They might have heard one or two laughing about the military defeats and disgraces that overwhelmed their troops wherever they went, inspiring even the bomb-shocked Londoners of the Blitz to sing:

> *What a surprise for the Duce, the Duce,*
> *He can't put it over the Greeks!*
> *What a surprise for the Duce, they do say*
> *He's had no spaghetti in weeks!*

They would have overheard the German soldiers joke, too, every bit as much as the British, about the number of reverse gears in Mussolini's tanks. One of General Rommel's chief interpreters, Wilfried Armbruster, had described them as a 'race of shits'. The Italians, in turn, would complain all the time about the advantages the German soldiers had over them – periods of leave and rest periods, superior equipment, the wholehearted support of the people back home.

There were those who were simply tired of fighting. Some of them had fought in Abyssinia, the land now known as Ethiopia. They knew the reality of the Great African Empire Mussolini had planned. Instead of a triumphant entrance through a major city told of and glorified in Fascist propaganda, they had borne witness to the mud huts of Addis Ababa and the gruelling poverty of the countryside around. They were aware of the use of poison gas, that Haile Selassi, the emperor of Ethiopia, was right in pointing out that 'from the end of January 1936, soldiers, women, children, cattle, rivers, lakes, and pastures were drenched continually with this deadly rain. In order to kill off systematically all living creatures, in order to more surely poison waters and pastures, the Italian command made its aircraft pass over and over again. That was its chief method of warfare.'

The Italian soldiers were also conscious of the reality of Libya. There might have been around 100,000 settlers occupying flat-roofed houses in towns like Benghazi, Derna and Tobruk, yet despite this, most of that country's deserts remained hostile. There were tribesmen like the Senussi whom Italian forces had ostensibly defeated. However, they waited out there and watched for Italians, intent on revenge if a soldier strayed too far from the main road.

In short, they were tired of all Mussolini's dreams and ambitions, doing their best to ignore the presence of his few remaining admirers in the camp still convinced by the truth of their Duce's vision. His words were now mimicked and parodied. They ridiculed his rhetoric the day he led them into conflict and promised 'We will conquer. And we will give finally a long period of peace with justice to Italy, to Europe and to the world.'

And so they tried to divert themselves, sitting within their desert tents, singing familiar songs in order to keep their spirits up. A few of these recall the war they have been involved in, like '*Sul Capello Che Noi Portiamo*', where they borrowed an Alpine soldier's song which boasts of the long black feather members of the regiment wear like a flag on their hats. 'Long live our regiment,' they chant from lips that must have contained more than a trace of irony, especially when few of these regiments served in the desert sand. Or '*Addio, Mia Bella Addio*', the title of a melody about a young man going off to war. 'I will not leave you alone,' he claims, 'But leave you a son to console you . . .' Or even one that ridiculed and poked fun at the whole notion of going to war:

> *Era nato poveretto*
> *senza casa e senza tetto.*
> *Ha venduto i suoi calzoni*
> *per un piatto di maccheroni.*
>
> *Tra la la la. Tra la la la.*
> *Tra la la la la la la la.*

Tra la la la la
Tra la la la la . . .

They traded stories too. A soldier from Milan told the tale of a particular game of billiards from his home region, one in which a young man plays a game against the king of the sun. He wins the hand of the monarch's daughter in marriage as a result of the contest. Some of his audience smiled broadly as they listened to this tale. They love this sport and are delighted that a fellow enthusiast won the opportunity to marry a member of such a prominent family. 'Pot black!' a listener shouted in delight as the young couple elope together, escaping from the father's fiery temper and control.

The storyteller's voice faded away as he looked up at his listeners. Most of them were men from inland towns and farms with no knowledge of islands or the sea. They longed to get back to all they had left behind.

Nearby, Domenico Chiocchetti, a painter, sat and watched them, drawing the faces of these soldiers on a piece of paper he had found. The youngest of twelve children of a peasant family, this small, well-rounded man with dark curly hair had been born on 15 May 1910 in the village of Sorte and brought up in a small town called Moena nearby, in the Dolomites in the Trentino-Alto Adige or South Tyrol area in the north-east of Italy. After that, he had gone to work in a studio in Ortisei, another town in the region, known for its woodcarving and beautiful, ornate churches. He had attended technical school in Ortisei, studying the art of painting statues and decorative work – a craft he put into practice in a number of churches such as the main town, Bolzano, or the village of Laste in Belluno where he went in 1939. He worked there, frequently walking for miles across the heights and depths of the Dolomites to go from place to place, until a short time before Il Duce stepped out on the balcony to declare war. In June he was called up, becoming part of the 6th

Anti-Aircraft Regiment of the Mantua division, a particularly ill-equipped and not fully motorised force, bound for Libya. This happened as a result of his 6 months of national service in 1931 – a shorter period than the usual 18 months due to the fact that he was the youngest in the family – and occasional, short periods after that.

His war did not last long. An injury to his hand kept him in Mantua, delaying his embarkation on a ship bound for Bengasi at Naples. He spent much of that voyage drawing the faces of the men who were with him on that voyage, listening to their songs and smoking while he sketched their expressions. He might too have drawn the gulls that followed them out of the harbour, providing their feathers with unusual colours, the shades of the Italian flag perhaps, as he, a man from far inland, tried to make sense of his new surroundings, so unusual to him. Even when he arrived on the continent of Africa, he stayed behind the Front, doing his work as a copyist and graphic artist in one of the offices. On one of the few occasions he stepped out of the office, he was sent out for a whole week. Clutching a telescope and compass, it was his task to notify officers by phone of the flight paths of the warplanes overhead.

Only six months in the continent of Africa had passed when he was captured by the Allies; he hadn't even fired a shot. He might have been one of the 27,000 Italian soldiers trapped and held after their opponents launched a successful attack on Tobruk on 21 January 1941, overrunning the Libyan port in two short, dramatic days. He may have been one of a number sent to a prison camp near Tobruk. Its torments were described by fellow prisoner Luigi Bortolotti in his war diary. Bortolotti estimated that as many as 40,000 extremely thirsty and hungry Italian POWs, including himself, were squeezed into the 600–square-metre camp.* He writes of:

---

* By the beginning of February 1941, some 130,000 Italian troops had been captured in the battlefields of Sidi Barrani, Bardia and Tobruk.

Screams everywhere. Some are looking for their brother, others their cousin or someone from their village. A priest shouting and invoking the Almighty assures everyone that they'll soon give us food and water, and runs to answer every call, offering words of comfort to us all. There was such bedlam that we didn't manage to get to the food distribution in time. Will we get out of this unscathed? Lots of gunfire to keep the mass of men under control. They shot one soldier as he was trying to get through the barbed wire. He probably wanted to go and look for food.

It was not the only sign of indifference to the prisoners' suffering. Bortolotti, an educated man who eventually settled in Australia, noted some of the guards who were eventually to become his fellow nationals 'surreptitiously mingling with the mass of Italians, taking possession of watches, money, and even photographs of the men's relatives, as well as rings, including wedding rings and other valuables.' Like others, he bears witness, too, to the way some of the drunken wardens humiliated their charges, acting with them as 'shepherds with their sheep'.

After his time there, Domenico Chiocchetti was probably among the men sent to the camp at Geneifa, walking in its direction for two days and nights goaded by guns and guards. It covered a huge area stretching around the Great Bitter Lake, a saltwater lake between the north and south end of the Suez Canal. As well as Italians, it held nationals from Palestine, France, Cyprus, Australia and India. Only the Italians, however, were there as prisoners, crammed in a large compound. The New Zealand historian Frazer D. Norton describes the Italians as 'a happy and contented lot', who spent much of their time making models of famous buildings from sand and shells, 'proof,' he declares, 'of their craftsmanship' and evidence, too, of the skill they would display in captivity, transforming everyday objects into works of artistry.

Happiness and contentment were not how most men remembered it. Dust and flies cloaked their surroundings. The water supply was salty. Dysentery and heatstroke were common. It was a place where Domenico's stomach must have echoed with hunger, desperate, like most of the others, for food. It was, perhaps, to distract him from this that he spent more and more time drawing while his exile passed in Egypt, sketching the thorny acacia and palm trees he had seen from time to time in the desert, using any stub of pencil he could discover, thrown away, perhaps, by one of the guards. There were occasions when he would pick up scarab beetles, dragonflies and locusts that he came across, marvelling at the strangeness and intricacy of God's creation, thinking about how much was different from his surroundings at home. Or else he would lift up seashells, harsh and jagged on his feet if he ever stepped near the Great Bitter Lake. Again, he would try to capture each aspect of its appearance on any piece of wood or paper he could find. It was a way of escaping the terrible realities of the world in which he had found himself, the dirt and squalor that was all around.

The day came when his drawing brought its own peculiar reward. An interpreter approached the men and spoke. 'I think we may have work for some of you,' he said. 'We're looking for artists among the prisoners.'

For a moment, no one stood or answered.

'They will receive extra rations, of course, if they volunteer for the task.'

The painter's neighbour nudged the small, slight figure with his elbow, mouthing words out of the edge of his mouth. 'That's a job for the likes of you, Domenico . . .'

'Are you sure?' he asked, conscious of the horrors that had been perpetrated by some of their guards. He wasn't certain he wanted to get into any closer proximity to them.

'Yes. Take the risk,' his fellow soldier muttered, perhaps parodying the slogan 'Better to live one day as a lion . . .'

'All right.'

Slowly, Domenico raised his hand.

༈

In a country far to the north and considerably colder than Egypt, another man noted for his care and diligence continues to carry out his work. Jim Nicolson planed and sawed the wood he had been given, showing a meticulous attention to detail rarely found in young men. He worked beside the stretch of ocean where he had spent most of his life, a much greater stretch of salt water than the Great Bitter Lake. It is large and wide enough to keep the *Almanzora* afloat. A 16,000-ton liner chartered for the purpose of housing the men who are needed at the camp, it dwarfed all that surrounded it from 11 May 1940 to the following November, when it lifted anchor and set sail once again. During its time there, it served many purposes. Its holds were full of the materials required for the task ahead, brought to shore by 'the six steam drifters', which were, as noted by Alastair and Anne Cormack, 'tendered to the ship and berthed overnight at St Mary's pier'. In contrast, supplies came to St Mary's pier and the south side of Burray by more orthodox methods for all that they were unloaded in less conventional ways elsewhere.

The *Almanzora* also provided berths of its own, giving living accommodation to the men of the Admiralty on its starboard side, and those from Balfour Beatty on the port side. There they planned and gave shape to Churchill's orders, the brusque command still ringing in their ears. It provided them, too, with little luxuries, tiny compensations for the months they were to spend far from home. Wine waiters and stewards passed among them, moving through the liner's gracious dining rooms, catering for their every whim and need. Particularly in the context of ration-book Britain that existed elsewhere, these portions were on the generous side. There were only 150 workers on board, but in the six months the liner was anchored in its place there were enough provisions on board for 1,000 men.

Despite all this, there was a chorus of complaints from the workforce. Before the first fortnight had passed some 70 men had rediscovered a great attachment to their homes in England and demanded to be sent back there. Bowing under the sheer weight of moans and grumbles, the officials had little choice but to give in to them. 'They're all troublemakers,' they told themselves. 'The best men are in the services and we're left with the rabble.'

However crudely this view might have been expressed, there was some truth in the statement. In the aftermath of the Hungry Thirties, many were part of that lost generation who had no opportunity to gain any familiarity with the discipline and routine required of men in a full-time job of work. It would have been difficult for them to adjust to its demands anywhere but at this particular time, the landscape of Orkney must have seemed surreal, almost a fantasyland to them. To begin with, it was rural, bereft of the type of housing they had known all their lives. It lay by the sea, complete with the long, stretches of sand some had only glimpsed in the saucy postcards their friends might have sent from their holidays in Blackpool or Skegness. ('Where's the bleeding donkeys?' one or two of them might have asked. 'Where are the puppets? Where's all the ice cream?') There was also – as midsummer approached – that endless, unerring daylight, impossible to find sleep in, chilling to those whose horizons had in the past been narrowed by a tenement building or a long stretch of terraced housing.

It was also a war zone. One of my informants, the spry and energetic octogenarian Ron Marwick, recalled standing as a young boy with his father watching a display of shells and flares shading the horizon like some low-level version of the Aurora Borealis, or the Northern Lights, that the people of Orkney have witnessed for generations. Touched by its beauty, they failed to hear the drone of aircraft flying overhead. It was only when one skirted narrowly over the roof of their home that Ron looked up.

'And there it was. A Heinkel bomber. I could see one of its crewmen sitting in its cockpit, as close as you are to me . . .'

There were other ways, too, in which the war touched Ron's childhood. He spoke to me in his home, a converted church complete with belfry, about how – in addition to all the other workplaces – there used to be two big hangars in St Mary's where barrage balloons were made and filled with helium. Soon after the start of the war, these added their extraordinary elements to the wartime landscape of Orkney. While some sailed high above Burray and South Ronaldsay, others were tethered to around 20 fishing trawlers dotted around the waters nearby, an inflatable barrier against those members of the German Luftwaffe who flew in the direction of Scapa Flow and the island airbases. Together with his friend Alfie Hutcheon, young Ron used to go out to them on the supply drifter *Rachel Flett*, bringing them provisions of fresh food during their periods of being marooned at sea. 'It was great fun being a delivery boy,' he grins, lifting his fireside stool up with his feet. 'Great fun indeed.'

It was an errand that took place in a surreal period in Orkney's history. It was little wonder then that so many of the new recruits to the Barriers found it hard to settle there. It would have been a difficult task for many of them to cope with the customs and habits of work. Outside their usual environment, it would have been impossible.

Their discontent must have had its effect on native islanders too. Men like Jim Nicolson would have bristled each time he heard them curse and moan about the weather and remoteness, the emptiness of much of the landscape, even the endless light of midsummer approaching. As someone who discovered his Christian faith at an early age, he must have been particularly irritated by both the sentiments and language of a little song they used to sing about the island in wartime, created by a serviceman – rumoured to be a man called Captain Hamish Blair – who had the 'misfortune' to be in Orkney for a time:

This bloody town's a bloody cuss –
No bloody trains, no bloody bus,
And no one cares for bloody us,
In bloody Orkney.

The bloody roads are bloody bad,
The bloody folks are bloody mad,
They'd make the brightest bloody sad,
In bloody Orkney.

Everything's so bloody dear,
A bloody bob for bloody beer,
And is it good – no bloody fear,
In bloody Orkney . . .

Jim would shut his ears to all their oaths and swears, pretending not to hear them as they blended with the clanking and thrum of the engines that bustled all around him. He had long ago decided that, to use the quiet and understated words of his fellow islander Edwin Muir when he travelled around Scotland in 1955, Orkney represented 'the only desirable form of life that I found in all my journey'. He knew the problems of island life, both in Orkney and further north in Shetland, how sometimes people gossiped and bore false witness against one another. Most of the time, however, aside from these small lapses, they behaved with kindness and decency, displaying little considerations and virtues that a large number, particularly living in its cities, were without.

There were other reasons why he worked on the Barriers. He could see the virtues of their existence for the people of the islands. As local historian George Esson pointed out to me in his home in St Margaret's Hope, this was a time when travelling from Kirkwall to South Ronaldsay involved a boat journey from Scapa, with the voyage frequently proving impossible in the depths of winter.

Another rationale was provided by the existence of the blockships themselves. Their great and hulking presence had altered the surge and fall of the tides flowing through the channels. This already had tragic consequences for three people some years before. In March 1920, a boat with five occupants made its way from Burray to Holm. Their vessel capsized as it crossed Kirk Sound, drowning three: two men in their fifties, William Wooldrage and Andrew Sutherland, and a young girl of 16, Annie Robson from Hunda. In his statement, one of the survivors, William Budge from Burray, blamed their accident on the way the blockships sunk after the First World War had changed the currents in the Sound. Ironically, however, it was also these self-same ships that saved both his life and that of Edward Ritch from Deerness: Budge clung to one until he was spotted by a group of fishermen on shore; Edward Ritch was saved while stranded on the hulk. What made this act even more remarkable was, as *The Orcadian* reported: 'Budge was wounded whilst on service, and has partially lost the use of one of his arms.'

Yet there was little time to brood upon such thoughts in the endless turmoil of the worksite. As well as the Barriers, quays were being built, extending their long concrete arms into the channels between the islands. They enabled boats to land, delivering their precious cargoes to the various camps. Lorries lumbered up and down the road to St Mary's bearing loads of different kinds. Some carried rubble, caged in wire netting some 17 feet by 6 feet in dimension. Their trailers would be reversed and emptied onto the end of the thin strand of rock that was already reaching its way out into the narrowness of the channel. The wire netting would perform its task then, preventing the huddle of stones being washed out by the next rush of tide far into the North Sea. And all this created a foundation for what was to follow. There were five-ton blocks made in the Rockworks factory which stood in St Mary's where the Commodore Motel is today. Small locomotives based in that yard and not unlike those that linked the quarries to the worksite helped to shunt and shift the blocks along. The blocks were moved into place to be carried on the high wire of the Blondins, holding and hurtling them to the places in which they would be set. This happened, too, to the larger, ten-ton blocks which arrived in the back of Atkinson's lorries from Jock Hay's quarry in Tankerness, a few miles away. Again, they creaked and trundled down the road where they had been created and constructed, ready for the greatest test of all, the pounding of the sea.

A great deal of thought had gone into preparing them for that particular challenge. In university laboratories, they had set out large-scale models in a range of different patterns, layering the blocks in a variety of ways. 'Which design is best for withstanding the full impact of a storm?' they pondered, putting the pieces of their giant jigsaw together. One time they might bring the larger blocks together to form the Barriers' skin. On another occasion they might employ the smaller ones on the outside. They wondered if its 'wall' should be smooth and linked closely together or set down in a rough and haphazard pattern. Eventually, they put them in place in what can only be described as an orderly form of disorder. This allowed the sea to surge in and out of them, lessening the impact of the waves against their foundation of stone. In most cases, the five-ton blocks formed the outside, shielding and protecting all that lay within.

The bare statistics of all this are awe-inspiring: 500,000 tons of rock dumped upon the seabed; 70, 000 blocks cut, over 30 an hour, 1 every two minutes, 300 a day. They dominated the skyline as much as the *Almanzora*. Stacked in giant pyramids, they were left to 'cure' before they were set in place. Unlike normal stone blocks, salt water played a part in their creation. There was so much of it around, lapping near the edge of the Rockworks factory. Besides, they were going to have to be able to cope with an overwhelming onslaught of salt when they were finally in place.

And slowly but surely, despite all the difficulties they have with their workforce, the Barriers begin to take shape, the gap in Kirk Sound narrowing first of all, the others shortly afterwards.

It reminded one onlooker of the folk tale of how the hills in the highest of all Orkney's islands, Hoy, had been created. It was said that a giant over in Orkney's neighbouring mainland county of Caithness had wanted some good soil for a stretch of barren ground near his home. Seeing some in Orkney, just across the Pentland Firth, he had strode over to fill his caisie – or creel – with it, his load brimming over the top. On the way back home, a clump fell out to form the isle of Graemsay. A moment later, the rope tying his load to his back snapped. Tumbling downwards, his basket emptied his load into the sea, becoming the hills of Hoy. After that, he stamped home in disgust at his own actions, leaving his former burden where it had fallen, creating new peaks and contours in the Orkney landscape.

The new arrivals in Orkney were doing much the same with their engines and lorries, Blondins and cranes. It was almost as if it had slipped out of some creel these modern giants were creating, this thin trickle of soil and stone between Lamb Holm, Glimps Holm, Burray and South Ronaldsay. This time, it would enable ordinary mortals to step over channels and sea currents, shifting from one outcrop of land to the next.

～

In the midst of another kind of turmoil, it is the pencil in Domenico's fingers that begins to restore his spirits, stirring him into life once more.

It is as if he is in Ortisei, the place which he, like his fellow Ladin speakers, call Urtijei. He can imagine he is looking up at the blue-grey mountains of the Alpe di Siusi, perched high above the valley where the town stands. He can see once again the dense green woodlands of Rasciesca, so unlike the fly-blown, windblown landscape that surrounds him now. And then there are the voices. The tongues of the French, Arabs, Australians and even most of his fellow Italians can be whisked away if he disappears long enough into his art. Instead, he can hear the words, perhaps, of the Ladin people, perched upon this long-disputed, long fought-over edge of the nation they call Italy, creating their own music in his ears.

There are moments when he might even be in more specific places. Around the stove of his family home in Moena, lost in the ripples of their ordinary conversations, mesmerised and made content by the humdrum routines of everyday life. He can see the faces of his brothers and sisters, his old parents there once more. Or he could be in the parish church of Urtijei, learning his craft from his old friend the artist Viktor Pitscheider once again. Built in the last years of the eighteenth century, it was a church where prayers and rosaries had circled for generations. He remembers how the bells rang from its tower on days when a funeral had taken place. The whole town stilled and held its breath as the procession made its slow, winding way up the steepness of its streets; the coffin on a cart drawn by two large, black horses; the prayers for the dying on the mourners' lips. It was so unlike the quick, brusque way in which men met their end in Geneifa. A few furtive words were said before dirt was shovelled, covering their bodies. Their dignity was robbed from them along with their breath.

The voices of the faithful seemed to add their own grace and ornamentation to the wooden statues in that church, ones he copied and imitated when beginning his trade. He knows the work well, aware that it was mostly crafted by artists from the locality of Val Gardena, a short distance by railway from the town. There is St Anna, together with her daughter the Virgin Mary by her side, created by Anton Pitscheider; Josef Moroder-Lusenberg's painting of the Adoration of the Virgin looking down at the Child in her arms; the sculpture of the Saviour on the Cross fashioned by the skills of Franz Ruggaldier.

And then there is – in his view – the central glory of the church. He looks up at the central domes decorated by the brothers Josef and Franz Xaver Kirchebner. Among their works is a painting of Saint Agnes. The patron saint of girls, she stands with her arm outstretched against a red background on a wall, both graceful and resolute in defence of her gender. They were also responsible for the portraits of St Ulrich, patron saint of the town and the name of the place in German, the language spoken by a good number of its inhabitants.

It is the skills that Domenico learned in these places that he now employs in Geneifa. He copies and enlarges the photographs that the men give him of their loved ones back at home, making hundreds during their time there. It is work that he enjoys, reminding him of the presence of women and children both at home and in the world at large. His years at war had almost made him forget the fact of their existence, that their small graces and kindnesses are also part of the world he inhabits. When he is given well-thumbed pictures of sweethearts back home or living in some distant port, he is careful to grant their faces and figures something of the perfection and beauty he witnessed in the statues that he'd studied earlier in his life.

The young soldiers reward him well for this. They tell the Indian cook who prepares their food to put an extra portion on the little Italian artist's plate. They place a few extra Egyptian piastres in his palm. It is cash like this that helps to feed his hungry companions in his camp. Men like his friend Sergeant Pennisi are grateful for it; their stomachs benefiting from Domenico's skills.

Yet he cannot help but hear whispers that destroy his sense of calm. They puff and trouble his ear continually. He is not the only one to feel this way. He is conscious that the British and Australian forces who surround them suffer from an even greater sense of insecurity and fear. It is the overall war situation that has caused these feelings. By the autumn of 1940, the Germans are clearly in the ascendancy. A fleet of their aircraft gathers in Sicily, waiting for the moment when they will seek to bomb Malta, the little island in the Mediterranean on which their security depends, into submission. The guards who stand over them are all too aware that it might not be that long before Panzer tanks roll into Libya, Tunisia, Egypt.

Anticipating that event, there are already swastikas and Italian flags waving there. They decorate some of the windows in the streets of Cairo. Some of the shopkeepers and shoeshine boys are rude and insolent as they serve the Allied soldiers when they are off duty, making clear where their allegiance lies. They see in the anticipated invasion an opportunity for their country to become an independent state again – for all that the British authorities predict that it is far more likely to become part of Mussolini's expanding African Empire. They even spread the rumour that their opponents have prepared a victory stamp for that day of triumph, one that bears the portraits of Egypt's new conquerors, Messrs Hitler and Mussolini. It is not a tale that convinces everyone in the country. Two of Egypt's future leaders, Sadat and Nasser were among those arrested for plotting on behalf of the Germans and Italians.

There is no doubt that many of the Italian prisoners would have caught their mood of anxiety and doubt from their British guards. The rare ones they called the 'indomitables', hardline followers of Il Duce, would pick up on every whisper, using them to undermine the confidence of those supposed to watch over them.

'It will not be long before there will be a victory parade here,' they predict, turning on those who stand over them with their guns. 'And you will be a prisoner of the Afrika Korps. Soon, Il Duce will gain his revenge. The day will come when he'll ride his favourite charger through the streets of Cairo.'

These men spoke too to their fellow prisoners, trying to reassure them and restore their belief in the Fascist cause. 'This is just a small step backwards. The day will come when Il Duce will take a giant stride onwards once again. Have faith. Victory is not that far away.'

One man from Piedmont spoke of having seen Mussolini once near his home, describing how he had walked through the stubble of green fields, surrounded by a crowd of people who had come from all around to see and touch him. One of his secretaries stepped behind him, handing out 1,000-lire banknotes to those who looked most miserable and desperate. Children were lifted above heads in order to catch a glimpse of – or better still, be touched by – him. Black-cloaked nuns gathered, giving him fruit which he took unsmilingly, handing them over to those who accompanied him on his travels. 'He is like a god,' he concluded. 'How can such a man be defeated? He will return and destroy these foes.'

Some guards took heed of all this; a few deserting their posts in the general atmosphere of fear. Domenico watched their faces, taking note of their disquiet as he sat and sketched their features, aware of the lines of apprehension that had gathered there over recent months. A shadow below their eyes. A line around their mouths. Wrinkles creasing foreheads. A few might even have expressed their worries, finding in the artist's attentions an escape from all the concerns that had been occupying them for so long. It could even have been one of them who let slip the idea that the British were planning to send most of their Italian prisoners to India, trying to make sure that those they had captured remained that way, never turning their guns against Allied forces in any future campaigns. The mention of the location must have caused a tremble in his own fingers, making his pencil falter as it moved across the paper, causing a blur in the sketch he was creating.

'India?'

He knew that St Thomas had gone there. The apostle who had doubted that Christ's resurrection had ever taken place, putting his fingers into the open wound that was on the Saviour's side. The disciple had been martyred there, killed by an arrow.

'India?'

He knew, too, that it was a hot and fevered place where the sun reached temperatures he would never be able to withstand. A place where there were few of his or any Christian faith. He knew that the prospect of going there affected him in the same way it did so many of the others. It filled him with dread, causing him to brood for days. Eventually he went to speak to a guard he knew and trusted, a corporal from Scotland. He saw the man's brow furrow, noting his request. 'I'll see what I can do,' he said.

A day or two later, the corporal returned to him.

'You'll be going to England instead,' he announced.

'Thank you . . . Thank you . . .' he stammered. He knew that for all that England was cold and damp, he could survive there. After all, there were times in the Dolomites when snow lay thick on the mountains and valleys for months. He had coped with that time and time again. Such cold was native to him, not penetrating nerve and bone in the way that heat did, sapping all his strength.

'Thank you . . .' he said once again, but this time it was not to the corporal. On this occasion, he spoke these words to the Virgin, to Christ stretched out on his cross . . .

4

BARRIERS

AN ITALIAN POW CONTEMPLATES SEAWEED

There are days I pop
bladderwrack with fingers,
pretending they are grapes
that grow upon the vine

But then there is no wine
within these grapes I burst.
only the taste of salt
that does not take away my thirst,

But leaves my tongue bitter,
longing for the taste of home
where branches all hang heavy
and I do not rely on foam

To wash up this strange harvest
on which no man can rely,
for it brings no fullness to my mouth
and makes my throat turn dry.

Story and song did much to shield them on their long voyage to the UK, sailing around the Cape of Good Hope to avoid war-torn Mediterranean waters. They felt emboldened as they sang a love song to a lady called Angiolina when they were anchored in Durban in South Africa, declaring how much they were in love with her since the night they went dancing together.

> *O Angiolina, bella Angiolina.*
> *O Angiolina, bella Angiolina . . .*

One crooned as he led a chorus that echoed across the harbour, drawing everyone's attention to those who were imprisoned in the ship. It was almost as if it were designed to capture the attention of those Italians imprisoned in other parts of the world, such as Kenya, India and South Africa, reminding them of the places they had come from before the conflict had started.

By the time they had reached Africa's largest harbour, Freetown in Sierra Leone, another song had caught their attention, one that probably summed up their worst fears of the way their loved ones might be betraying them at home.

> *La Dosolina la va di sopra*
> *e la si mette al tavolino.*
> *La Dosolina la va di sopra*
> *e la si mette al tavolino . . .*

Its sadness brought its own alien note to that great port, silencing the African workers as they went about their labours, wondering what was going on.

And then, too, there were the stories they swapped with each other. The men from the larger towns and cities spoke of the movies they had seen – tales, perhaps, of Charlie Chaplin and Maurice Chevalier, the beauty of Garbo and Dietrich, tough men like Edward G. Robinson and James Cagney.

'You dirty rat,' one kept saying as he shuffled his shoulders, puzzling those, like Domenico, who came from more remote areas of the country.

And there was the prisoner from Milan who kept repeating the dying words of Edward G Robinson as he was gunned down by police in the film *Little Caesar* the instant any misfortune happened to occur to him: 'Mother of Mercy, is this the end of Rico?'

The countrymen and villagers always looked at each other when those from the big towns spoke like that. They saw it as proof of the madness that affected the people there, especially those who had left behind both the family and countryside to which they belonged. They were reminded of the tale about a Florentine who left home to see a little more of the world, and who ended up frenzied and disappointed by all he discovered. He had found himself in a giant's lair, fortunate to escape with only the loss of one of his fingers when his one-eyed prison guard stamped and flailed around him, desperate to clutch him in his fist.

Their own lives had shown them the dangers of travel. They remembered it so well – how they puffed their chests like the Florentine about to set out into the world the day they put on their uniforms for the first time.

'*DUCE! DUCE! DUCE!*' they had chanted, 'Believe! Obey! Fight!'

And then they had tasted the bitterness of defeat. The careless cruelties of their officers. The fly-plagued, wind-scorched desert. Even the alien motion of this sea often sent their stomachs heaving, filling their mouths with bitterness and bile. They did not belong in these places. Instead, their lives stemmed from and were part of their small mountain villages, tiny homesteads and farms. There were rooted, too, in the comforts of the churches to which they travelled every Sunday, the tales of faith they had heard at their fireside. There was the story which the scholar among the prisoners dismissed and rejected, claiming it was not part of the

Gospels. It told of how Jesus had asked his disciples to lift up stones as they wandered around Sicily. Lazy and mindful of his back, Peter had picked up the smallest one, only to discover that the Lord was planning to turn them into bread and the pebble he had chosen was not going to satisfy the largeness of his appetite. The next day, he had strained himself by carrying a huge boulder upon his shoulders; after he had sweated a mile or two he found out that all his efforts had been wasted. They were on the edge of a town with a number of bakeries. Jesus and the apostles would buy the bread there.

It was stories like these that men like Domenico appreciated. His faith had deepened since he had left the village of Moena. As men around him suffered and died, it had strengthened and sustained him, giving him the courage to continue battling against all that threatened and surrounded him in his life. He felt God was looking after him, that there was a reason why he was alive after all he had gone through. Perhaps there was a purpose to his existence, one he had barely even glimpsed yet.

He might have recalled all this when their vessel neared their destination in Liverpool, going through the successions of locks to reach their harbour. His artist's eye took in the three fine buildings he could see along its seafront. There was one with a dome like a great cathedral. Another looked as if it was a palazzo in his own country, fine and impressive. And then there was this tall structure, topped by a huge copper bird that looked as if it were peering down at them, inspecting the prisoners as they stood on the pier. He shivered a little under its gaze, feeling a chill that was not just caused by the raw, English wind, but, perhaps, too, by the jeers and insults of the dock workers, a litany of names.

'You are prisoners of the Crown,' a British officer announced, 'held under the protocols relating to prisoners of war under the Geneva Convention of 1929. While we will look after your comfort and safety when you are in our custody, we ask you to bear this in mind at all times.'

The rain began to lash down then, beginning a drum roll that was every bit as insistent as the rattle of the train they travelled on later, heading north through England and across the Scottish border. Much of it looked empty to them – a terrible, endless greyness. Sky merged with open fields; byres and barns could be glimpsed as they rushed past. It was to places like these that the majority of Italian prisoners had been sent. Bodies with grandiose names like the County War Agricultural Executive Committee had need of them – to help with the business of feeding the nation now that they could no longer depend on imports from abroad and had few labourers available to them to work on the land. As *The Times* declared on 1 August 1931, shortly after the arrival of the first group of prisoners, they were to be involved in 'ditching, draining, land reclamation, and general work under the Ministry of Agriculture'.

As they journeyed north, they no doubt believed that this was in store for them too, ignoring the fact that so many of them were tradesmen – painters like Domenico; Giovanni Scarponi the driver of a diesel locomotive; Palumbi, a metal worker; Micheloni, an electrician – and not men skilled at working on the land. They all looked out the window, mourning the muted shade of the light at this time of year this far north, how the landscape outside lacked the lushness of their homeland. Some dozed and half-slept, only waking when they arrived in the bustle of Waverley Station in Edinburgh. There were other Italians waiting for them there, obscured by smoke and steam. He heard a voice jeering at them as they were marshalled into line by a British officer.

'Eyties!'

It got worse as they marched along King George IV Bridge and towards the Royal Mile. Faces contorted with hate shouted abuse at them as they did so. Some did mock-Fascist salutes and spat on the street before them. Others performed extravagant crosses across their heads and shoulders. There were various yells, loud and angry.

'Macaroni munchers!'

'Spaghetti eaters!'

Dominico shielded himself in a number of ways from all of this. His eyes skirted over the fine buildings on either side, noting how the city was like a darker, greyer version of Bolzano with its turrets and towers, all signs of the many battles that had been fought there. He took refuge, too, by pretending the insults were not aimed at him. He was not wholly Italian but Ladin. He had rarely eaten pasta in his life. At his home in Moena, his noonday meal had been polenta with cheese, milk or butter, accompanied by a little sauerkraut. Potatoes, bread and barley had sometimes filled his plate. No. These words were fashioned to hurt those from further south, those unlike him who truly believed in Mussolini and his cause.

Yet he was glad when the gates of Edinburgh Castle were closed behind them. Like many of the other prisoners, he took the time to write to his family, something he had been unable to do while he had been moved around camps in the north of Africa. After that, he was grateful for sleep. His eyes were only opened again the following morning when the group was marched down to the station once more. They did this with bleary eyes, feeling lost and confused. This was especially the case with a number of them, like Guido DeBonis from San Polo dei Cavalieri near Rome, who had even been shipped to Australia before returning to the northern hemisphere again. Their heads swirled, their peace of mind levelled by the tiredness they were suffering, the early morning insults directed at them.

'To hell with Mussolini!'

'Il Duce is il idiot!'

Finally, they were met on the railway platform by Major Yates and the men of the Royal Pioneer Corps. It was their purpose to take the prisoners further north, through a landscape that was even more bleak and forbidding, hostile and terrifying in the extreme.

Somehow, the whisper came round the carriage that they were going to a place called Orkney. It was a place name no one had ever heard of. They rolled it around their mouths, catching its strange, exotic flavour. 'Orkney... Orkney... Orkney...'

'Perhaps that's where the orc comes from ...' the scholar in their midst declared, his eyes blinking in the half-light of this cold, Scottish winter.

'The orc?' they questioned.

'A frightened, legendary sea-beast.' He told them of Ariosto's great poem, *Orlando Furioso*, written back in the sixteenth century. There was mention there of Scotland, where one of the book's heroes, Rinaldo, had been washed ashore on the edge of the great Caledonian forest that had stood in that country until peat bogs had laid waste to its acres. There was also a story about Proteus, an old sea god who was the shepherd in charge of Neptune's flocks ...

'Go on ...' they urged him.

'It is said that in the northern seas, out beyond the setting sun, there's an island called Ebuda, a place where very few people now live. A beautiful princess stayed there, daughter of the island's king. Each day Proteus used to watch her walk its shoreline until he could stand it no more. He caught her alone one day. He embraced and ravished her where she stood and made her pregnant with his son. Her father, the king was so angry about this that he beheaded her, killing the baby, too, in her womb ...'

'I'm not sure I want to go there,' someone shivered.

They laughed at the Neapolitan who had spoken, teasing him for his gullibility. 'It's only a story,' they told him. 'Only a poem written centuries ago.'*

For all that, the tale didn't make them feel any more at ease by the time they arrived on the island. They did so by way of

---

* Scholarly readers may note that the author is being more than a little disingenuous here. Though the orc might have been resident there, 'Ebuda' is far more likely to be his native Hebrides than Orkney.

Aberdeen, Domenico glancing up at the buildings as he was marched with the other men down to the docks. Again, he took in the city's architecture, the smell of fish from its harbour. It looked a cold and artless place, the stone walls that surrounded him featureless and plain. It seemed the further north they went, the more bare and desolate the world became. He felt relieved to be leaving there, anxious to escape its hold.

After that, the 600 men were crowded onto a large, old railway packet steamer, one that normally sailed between England and the continent, crammed together in its darkness. They followed in the wake of a Royal Navy destroyer heading north to Scapa Flow. They anchored there. Finding their vessel too large to berth at the Warebanks pier in Burray, they disembarked in small boats. It was as they did this that they took in their surroundings for the first time. The bleakness and flatness. The small, cramped limits of an island world, so unlike the towns and villages they had left. There were rivers in their homeland like those Ungaretti praised in his verse:

> . . . the Serchio
> which has given water
> for two thousand years maybe
> to my peasant people
> to my father and my mother.

In this landscape, by contrast, there was barely a proper stream where fresh water could trickle through their fingers, no trees to provide them with shade or shelter. Their mood did not lift when a few days later, they were on the move once more, stepping onto a fishing boat that took them across to Lamb Holm.

Peter Norn Kirkness from Burray sat astride the saddle of the new 'Rudge' bicycle he'd obtained through his work with Balfour Beatty and watched the men line up on the pier that day. A young lad at the time, he sensed the misery that lay behind their dark, tanned skin, burnished by the hot desert sun. They 'seemed to be feeling the cold,' he noted, observing how they shivered. 'Many wore cloth capes instead of greatcoats.'

Yet the chill went deeper than the outward shake and tremble, unable to be stilled or stopped by the tight wrapping of a coat. Instead, their despair travelled deep to their core, filling them with the sense of hopelessness recalled by Domenico in an article he wrote for *The Orcadian* in 7 December 1960, describing how the little island of Lamb Holm 'could hardly have appeared more desolate: bare, foggy, exposed to the wind and heavy rain.'*

Then there was the accommodation he could see in the distance. Again there is a bare description. Overlooking the fact that it had – in Sergeant Slater's words in *Churchill's Prisoners* – 'to be secured against the gales by steel staywires fastened at the sides by concrete', Domenico simply writes that 'the camp consisted of thirteen dark, empty huts and mud'.

Glancing round, the Italian prisoners took it all in. The barbed wire around the huts on an island empty of houses. The alien, almost Arctic landscape, bare of tree or bush. The waves racing and tumbling over each other, as if they were gathering together to make this island even more flat and level than it was already, concealing it below the tumult of the sea. The bustle of the men all around them working in mud and dirt, driving lorries and rail engines, pitched high in their cranes, the wind singing through the steel girders of their platforms. The hoots and shouts and clank of metal. To their eyes, there seemed something almost inhuman in this landscape. They looked to the ocean for signs of sea monsters. There was scarcely a single 'idler or vagabond' in sight – a fact that made the more lazy ones among them come to the same conclusion as Pinocchio: 'I see that this island will never suit me! I wasn't born to work.'

The few indomitables among them came to a different conclu-

---

* Most accounts allege they arrived in Orkney in January, though some – like that of Bruno Volpi, for instance – claim this did not occur till the end of February.

sion. They looked out at those who guarded them with contempt, seeing an island race that was about to be choked and defeated by the ring of steel their Axis forces had forged around them. Didn't the streets of Paris now echo with the sounds of German tanks? Wasn't the beat of jackboots to be heard in Oslo and Copenhagen? Weren't the Luftwaffe – high and triumphant – to be seen above Prague and Warsaw? Wasn't it even the case that in the very battlegrounds where they had been trapped and captured, Rommel and his Panzer tanks now held sway? There had been moments when they doubted it but their old beliefs had been proved true yet again. '*Mussolini ha sempre ragione.* Mussolini is always right.' What they had thought were defeats were only 'tactical withdrawals', allowing their forces to gather strength once again, sealing the frontiers of his European empire.

And so they had to keep faith. The 'long period of peace with justice, to Europe and to the world' Mussolini had promised the evening he stood on that balcony in Rome, declaring war on the Allies, could only come to pass if men like them, his people, showed their tenacity and worth.

'*Viva Il Duce! Viva Il Camerata!*' they shouted.

Their voices rippled out in the cold January air, as raucous as the wind that howled around them. Something froze within the other prisoners as they heard those who were Fascists shout their slogans. For a few, it was a reminder of the old verities, the faith they had for so long in Mussolini and his cause. Forgotten for a time, its certainties stirred within them once again. They remembered words scrawled upon the walls of their small towns and cities, how it was 'better to live one day as a lion than a thousand years as a sheep'. Convinced again that all this might be true, their heels clicked together. Their backbones stiffened.

For others, there was a frisson of fear, a reminder that they had wives, families, children at home. When they were sure that no Fascists were present, most of them spoke of Mussolini as the '*Puzzone*', the 'smelly one', his government fit only for '*canalins*', dogs. However, if word ever got home that they had been disloyal to Il Duce and all his dreams and ambitions, it might not be long before their houses were visited by a Blackshirt. There would be a rap at their door, a blow from a fist or jackboot. They were determined to avoid this happening, for the wrath of the Fascists to be visited on their kin.

'*Viva Il Duce! Viva Il Camerata!*' they shouted.

And then there were men like Domenico Chiocchetti. He did what men from his community had done for centuries – say as little as possible when those around him spoke about their nation, flag and state. After all, he never thought of himself as wholly 'Italian'. His first tongue, Ladin, was one derived from a rough version of Latin spoken by the ordinary Roman soldiers and merchants who had arrived in the Dolomites, influenced, too, by the local tongues and dialects of that area. The fall of the Roman Empire in the fifth century had left the language exposed, changing further as it grew more and more confined to isolated areas like the town of Moena in the Fassa valley where Domenico grew up. Nevertheless, he probably pretended to sing the words of '*Vincere*' that had bound the troops together the first days they had put on their uniforms and set out in the direction of their leader's Field of Miracles.

> *Temprata da mille passioni*
> *La voce d'Italia squillò:*
> *'Centurie, Coorti, Legioni*
> *In piedi che l'ora suonò!'*

Some of the Balfour Beatty men who looked on must have experienced a terrible sense of foreboding when they heard that anthem being sung. It was true that they were making good progress; the Barriers were far ahead of where they had ever dreamed they might be at this stage in proceedings. However, they had gone through a great deal of trouble with their labour force. Many of their first recruits had – as has been noted before

– not coped well with the extremes of the island's climate. Despite a scheme known as the 'Orkney Agreement', by which men who signed on for three months received a period of paid leave, they had been unable to retain many of their workforce. As the war shifted south, so had they, working instead on the defences needed for the south-east of England – an area of the country receiving the kind of attention from the Luftwaffe Orkney had obtained during an earlier period of the conflict. There was also conscription, the arrival of call-up papers forcing many men to exchange their work clothes for a uniform.

And then there had been the Irish men. During my time in his home, Ron Marwick recalled how their behaviour had caused the people of Holm more than a little concern. 'Some of them spent their Saturday nights drinking and fighting. It wasn't too bad. No one would have said anything about it on a Friday night in Sauchiehall Street. But no one drank in Holm at that time. No one at all.' He chuckled at a memory. 'I remember a fellow called Big Jimmy McKinnon saying he was going to get this other fellow called McGarvie. "I'm going to kill McGarvie," he kept yelling, "I'm going to get him."'

There were, however, more serious matters for the authorities to think about than an occasional skirmish on a Saturday night. Trying to take advantage of what they saw as 'England's local difficulty', the IRA launched one of its periodic local campaigns both north and south of the Irish border. Men were killed; targets chosen. A statement from the IRA announced that they were quite prepared to collaborate with the German government in order to achieve the goal of Ireland's freedom.

And then there was the matter of a few pro-IRA slogans appearing in the worksite. '*Tiocfaidh ar la!*' (Our day will come!) scrawled on the wall of a Nissen hut; 'IRA forever' elsewhere.

There is no doubt that those who were in charge of the Barriers became nervous at the sight of all this. They could foresee all their hard work being sabotaged. A few sticks of dynamite could go missing from one of the quarries – Moss, perhaps, or Links or Warebanks on Burray – and a Royal Navy ship could be trapped under fathoms of water in Scapa Flow. Or, perhaps, one of the airfields could be their target, its runway undermined by this 'enemy within' rendering it inoperable for months. They decided that there was no choice but to send many of Irish men away from Orkney. The safety of both the realm and the Barriers demanded that this action had to take place. It was defended by no less a person than the former First Lord of the Admiralty, Sir Winston Churchill, who in May 1941 wrote:'it might be better to use these docile Italian prisoners of war instead of bringing in disaffected Irish, over whom we have nothing like the same control.'

Yet there was nothing docile about Italian men. The only difference between them and the Irish seemed to be in terms of politics. They were yet another group of people who were hostile to Britain and its war aims. The native Orcadians could only listen with alarm as Mussolini's slogans rang out across Kirk Sound, watching these men make their way to Camp 60 in Lamb Holm, Camp 34 in the island of Burray, the row of Nissen huts that would provide a bleak and comfortless home for the prisoners until the final battle had been fought and won. Picking up both heat and tempo, slipping occasionally through mud and puddles, they sang their song again.

> *Temprata da mille passioni*
> *La voce d'Italia squillò . . .*

The Italian prisoners on Orkney were not the only ones to respond to captivity in a belligerent way.

In his diary, Bortolloti regrets that while suffering the indignity of being a prisoner of war in Australia, he was unable to commit the 'ultimate sacrifice' for his 'beloved country'. He welcomes, too, the attack on Pearl Harbour, noting with pleasure their ally's 'brilliant naval victory in its first day in the war'. Even Hitler's series of defeats in Russia at a later stage in the conflict do little to endanger his confidence in the eventual outcome of the war. 'I still have complete faith in our victory,' he declares, 'Nothing will make me lose heart.'

And then there are the escape attempts he celebrates in his writing. He records the fact that there were a number of tunnels burrowed under the camps, one of them extending 150 metres beyond the barbed wire. Two prisoners escape in civilian dress and are caught two hours later. Another pair survive outside for two days before they are found, hungry and dishevelled, once again. There was even the tale of Lieutenant Edgardo Simoni who managed to escape on two occasions – once for 11 months.

A different kind of defiance, however, was displayed by some of the men in Orkney during their early days of imprisonment. In the beginning, they seemed quiet and settled. No doubt grateful for an end to their journey, they appeared content with the prospect of being fed once again, the warmth of sheets and blankets, even a world that no longer shifted and swayed from side like the hull of a boat. There was also an acceptance of the realities of their captivity. There was no outback to which they could run, no nearby town to which they could disappear. And then, too, there were some who felt chastened by the humiliation of defeat. They felt sorry for themselves, wishing the call of adventure had not enticed them into leaving their homes.

One or two even muttered to themselves about how well they were being treated in the camp compared to how their own officers had acted in the desert, taking the greater share of the food. 'They are showing us more kindness than those of our own blood.'

And then this altered – the whispers of the few indomitables the British had not weeded out strengthening both backbone and resistance. They talked about how an Axis victory was assured in the long run, that this was just a temporary setback for them. Even if they were imprisoned for a time, it would not be long till they were free and restored to their homes. For those who had long accepted that 'Mussolini was always right', this was the restoration of a familiar credo. For those who did not, there was the fear that any anti-Fascist statement they made would reach the authorities in Italy and this would have what Sponza in his book, *Divided Loyalties* describes as 'unpleasant consequences for their families' back home.

As a result, they all stood and listened while the indomitables argued over the work that the Canadian officer-in-charge, Major Yates, had asked them to do – this strange, stone Barrier that the reviled warmonger Winston Churchill wanted them to create.

'We are not going to work on this . . .' they declared.

'Why not . . .?'

'We are helping the British in the war. This is not allowed! We would be betraying our country if we did this.'

'Not only that . . . But if we work here, we're in danger of being killed by our own side . . . The Germans' planes won't stop if they think we're Italians. In fact, some of them will be even more determined to kill us if they think we're Italians.'

'No doubt about that,' one man from Trento laughed wryly, recalling the many quarrels with the Germans they had seen in his region over the years. On the one side, there were men like Peter Hofer, the master tailor who led the VKS, the party that wanted to stitch up the entire Alto Adige within the borders of Hitler's Thousand Year Reich. On the other, Benito Mussolini with his dreams of a new Roman Empire. Grinning, he pointed out the red cloth that was sewn upon the back, behind the elbows and on the knees of their prisoner-of-war uniform in order to prevent them escaping. 'Look! The British have even put targets on our clothes. Just to be as helpful as they can.'

'Men of Rustic Honour,' the scholar joked, referring to Mascagni's opera, *Cavalleria Rusticana*.

'It won't be rust that'll be turning us red if we step out there when the Luftwaffe are around.'

'*Viva, il vino spumeggiante!*'

Ignoring the hubbub of voices in the hut, one of the Italian officers, Fornasier, turned towards Domenico, jerking his head in the direction of the door. 'Let's go and have a word together.'

Domenico did as he asked, inhaling from his cigarette as he stood in the open doorway of the hut, dominated by the taller, broader man at his side.

'If we're going to object to this work, we'll need evidence. Otherwise, no one will listen to a word we'll say.'

'Evidence?' Domenico asked. 'How will we get that?'

'Come with me...'

The two of them walked in the direction of the highest point of the tiny island. It was a rare still day, the first since they had arrived, and he could see the row of houses on the Orkney mainland, facing Lamb Holm. They were bereft of the light and shade he saw among the houses of his homeland. No murals etched upon the wall. No red roofs. Only dull, grey stone. Around him, too, there was the flotilla of ships at anchor in the Flow, a few more a short distance from where they stood. He could also see the barrage balloons fastened to the fishing boats, creating a maze for German planes to weave their way through if they were going to attack the channels between the islands or even beyond. They were their main defences – if anything might stop the red targets on their clothing being transformed into bloody wounds.

'I want you to draw all this,' Fornasier said.

Domenico looked over towards Guerrino Fornasier, taking in every detail of his furrowed forehead, his swept-back brown hair, his pencil-thin moustache. 'Why?'

'It will prove what we are saying. That we are working on something that is connected to the war.'

'All right...' He nodded his head, obeying the young man who was his superior. The two of them walked slowly, tentatively, back to the huts, aware that their every step was treacherous in the dampness of the grass.

His fingers clutching a few sheets of paper and a piece of

board, Domenico was back on the hillock a short time later, sketching the outline of the scene with his pencil. The hills are low and gently rounded, mirrored in the stillness of the sea. There was nothing of the magnificence of the mountains that surrounded him in the Dolomites. The hills did not flare and grow red with the sunset. Instead, the flatness of the ground was quiet and muted at this time of the year as it sank slowly into the sea.

He looked for the peace of God, *Pax Dei*, in the scene. It seemed to have been driven out by these other presences he was forced to include in this picture. The grey warships in the harbour. Barrage balloons. A plane taking off bristling with weapons. The ugliness of machines brought to these shores to build the Barriers. Sometimes he thought that the purpose of his artwork had changed beyond recognition since he first put on a uniform. He spent his time sketching weapons and aircraft, the dark and hidden interior of an engine or a gun. He wanted his fingers to unfold once again those signs and symbols he had drawn before the war. A dove. Angels. St Joseph and St Francis. St James. The picture of the Madonna of the Olives he still kept within his pocket with the following words printed on the other side:

> Oh Jesus you said: 'I have come to bring the fire (of charity) to the earth, and what else do I want if not that it be kindled?' Oh, let men, overcoming individual and national egoism, recognise themselves as brothers. May they refrain from discord. May they love and help one another and form one heart with Your heart in loving, praising and blessing the common Father who is in heaven, to whom is all honour and glory now and for ever. Amen.

ॐ

'You have told us that we are held under the protocols relating to prisoners of war under the Geneva Convention of 1929. Within this document, it states that no prisoner of war can perform any task which might help their opponents' war effort. We believe that working on the Barriers is like this. It is against all the rules that govern modern warfare.'

It was the interpreter who had spoken, translating every word from Fornasier's lips.

'Nonsense,' Major Yates snapped. A brisk, rude Canadian, he had little time or patience for the arguments of the Italians. And little respect for them, given how badly they had fought in the war. He was distracted by a discussion that was going on just outside his office, the words seeping in under the doorway. Someone squints outside to see a small, dark-haired man shouting and yelling in a language he could not even begin understand. 'What's he saying?' he asked Fornasier.

The interpreter fired the question in Fornasier's direction.

The tall, dark haired Italian shrugged. '*Non capisco*,' he said.

'We could find out. Can't the man speak any English?' he growled in the direction of the interpreter.

The interpreter shook his head, looking at him in complete frustration. 'I don't think he can even speak Italian,' he replied. 'Or not very well anyway. A peasant dialect.'

'Oh . . . That's probably why they can't fight well together. Too many different languages.' He glanced up at MacAulay, a dark-haired Hebridean from North Uist. 'Not like us, eh? We all speak the same lingo. Don't we?'

'Yes, sir. *Gu dearbha*. That's for sure.'

Yates paused for a moment, considering his remark before looking once more at the men who stood before him. 'You wouldn't have been sent here if what you were saying was true. Are you suggesting the British government is breaking international law?'

'Yes. I am. Both these men . . .' He gestured towards Domenico and the others, 'and those imprisoned on the other island think that.'

'Burray.' Yates informed him of the other island's name. 'And what are you asking me to do about it?'

'Report our demands to your superiors. We want you to move us to somewhere safer, somewhere less warlike than here.' He brandished Domenico's drawings before the major's face. 'We want the arrangements for this to be done within a week. Otherwise, all work will stop.'

'You're sure about this? It seems to me that you're acting very unwisely.'

'*Si.* I am sure.'

'All right . . .'

There is a flurry of paper, the sound of someone muttering. 'Mussolini very good man. Churchill very bad man.'

Yates seems to register the words, fixing the men with a searching glare. It is an age before he lets them go. 'I will forward your complaint to your Protecting Power, the Swiss representative in London. They will let me know their view on this eventually.'

'When will that be?' Fornasier asked.

'I don't know the answer to that one. I am not a prophet. In the meantime, I suggest that you continue work upon this construction. It would be in your interest to do so.'

'*Ma va* . . . No way,' one of the Fascists at the rear of the room whispers.

Again the major hears, smiling wryly in response. 'Of course. I've heard that's your philosophy. "Better to live one day as a lion than a hundred years as a sheep." Well, we'll see about that . . .'

The office clock ticks as he looks around the room. They can hear a lorry splashing through one of many pools of water on the site, soaking a worker who swears and yells in the vehicle's direction.

'You are dismissed,' the major finally declares.

As they leave that office, moving across the camp, Domenico tells himself that they are right in taking this stand. There is no doubt that the British are breaking international law in the way they are acting, a strange form of behaviour for a nation that always tells itself it has a reputation for following rules.

Yet at the same time, he feels tired and fed up of all this arguing. Throughout much of his life, he had stepped across a precarious landscape, one created by politicians and other men much more powerful than him. It all reminded him of the way dolomite, the rock that surrounded his home, was described by a French geologist who had stayed in his parents' *pension* in Moena. A young, serious-minded man, he had turned a piece of rock round and round in his fingers. 'Dolomite is the thick caprock we see on the surface,' he said, 'Underneath it, we can find shale. That's just clay turned into fine, grey rock. Water works through the dolomite and when it gets to the shale it just lies there. It's unable to get through the thin layers and fine grain. As a result of this, guess what happens? The erosion that destroys the dolomites works its way back to the source, eating its way through the channel. As a result of that, the caprock develops vertical joints. *Capeesh?*'

He pronounced the Italian word the way many foreigners did. Domenico nodded, still tired from having walked much of the distance between Ortisei where he worked and his home. With the unreliability of public transport, he had no choice but to do that.

'It's not long before these weak vertical joints lean out and leave crevasses between them. After hundreds, perhaps thousands, of years they break off altogether and go tumbling down the slope.'

'Like the Hapsburgs,' one of his friends joked, recalling the monarchs of the Austro-Hungarian Empire who had ruled over the South Tyrol for generations.

'Like all politicians,' the Frenchman smiled. 'Even those found in my country.'

Within the prison camp, he could see much of that in the few remaining Fascists who were near him. Some of them were with them in the huts set aside for staff, living in places where only 15 men could sleep. Others were in the larger huts for 50 or so. They all, though, had some things in common. Their shoulders all seemed as broad as some of the crests of the Dolomites in his homeland, their huge chests jutting out into everyone else's airspace and looming over all those who were with them in the camp. He could see this when they waited for the answer to come from the Protecting Power. It didn't matter that they, like Yates, had told the prisoners to keep working till the decision was made.

'We will not do it,' one of the leading Fascists in the camp had declared. '*Chi osa vince . . .* Who dares wins.'

'*Boia chi molla . . .* To hell with those who give up,' his friend muttered.

'*Beffo la morte e ghigno . . .* I mock death and grin,' another parroted one more phrase beloved of the Blackshirts.

Grinning was something Domenico did not feel like doing when Yates began to punish the men for their actions. Ordering the prisoners to line up before him that afternoon, he stood there and told them what he was going to do. The cold wet sleet cut through their clothing as they listened to him speak.

'You are going to be placed on a 14-day punishment diet. This will be bread and water each day. Normal rations every fourth day . . .'

His jawline jutted out from his shirt collar as he said this. His hands were on his hips and his legs splayed apart in a pose that seemed vaguely familiar to them all. There was even his deep, sonorous voice as he announced his decision. Barely had the words came out of his mouth than there arose a loud, repetitive chant that must have sounded like the one heard outside Palazzo Venezia when Mussolini had declared war on the Abyssinians.

'*DUCE! DUCE! DUCE!* Believe! Obey! Fight!'

He looked at them calmly as they shouted in his direction, not acknowledging their defiance. Only his hands betrayed his feelings, tightening into fists.

ॐ

Major Yates' fingers were not the only ones to be clenching.

It was also true of many of Domenico's fellow prisoners. He could feel that mood was in them. The tensing of muscles. The grinding of teeth. It was something he had become well attuned to during his time in places like the Central Railway Station in Bolzano with its monolithic towers, its reminders of Imperial Rome. The latter was a place where many were hushed into silence. The naked sculptures near its entrance seemed to speak of all of Il Duce's brute force and power, reminding those who travelled on journeys below them which individual was always in charge here.

The guards were feeling the same way. He could sense that in the stiffness of their stance, how their hands held a tight grip on their rifles. He had heard them muttering threats, too, as they doled out the bread and water that was to be their meagre meal.

'Think Churchill's going to let you off with this?' one muttered, turning his fingers in that famous 'V-sign' towards them. 'Bloody Eyties. Dagos . . . He'll show you.'

The few Fascists among them responded with their own gestures, raising their hands in a salute, muttering, too, that expression so many of them loved. 'Believe . . . Obey . . . Fight . . .'

There were a number who went further in their opposition. First of all, there were small gestures of defiance. Spittle starring the back of a guard when he passed by in the camp. A poster ripped down. Taps left running. It reached its worst moment when a couple of Fascists broke into the cookhouse, spilling on the floor pans full of the food they were not going to be allowed to eat on the floor. Together with some of the other indomitables, they were taken away by armed guards. Rumours travelled round the camp that they were going somewhere even more northerly, to be imprisoned along with the most recalcitrant Nazis.

'Shetland . . .' one of the guards whispered, 'You'd almost feel sorry for the poor wee souls.'

Their disappearance did not lessen the tension. That continued even after those most obedient to Mussolini had been taken from their company. The prisoners quarrelled among themselves, their local, regional loyalties permitting them to spit and argue with those who came from the opposite end of the country. The men from Trento fought with those from Rome. In one of the huts, some prisoners from Calabria had grown tired of insults about how remote and backward their part of southern Italy was and struck out with toes and boots, fighting with those who shared their living space. Domenico had overheard a few remarks about his homeland. Someone had claimed the people there weren't really Italian. 'It's all sausage-eaters up there, polluting the Alto Adige. Sooner we get rid of them the better . . .'

A few of his fellow officers used to chide the other prisoners when they came out with remarks like that, reminding them of the words of the 'Giovinezza':

> Dell'Italia nel confine
> Son rifatti gli Italiani
> Li ha rifatti Mussolini
> Per la Guerra di domani . . .

> In the Italian borders,
> Italians have been remade.
> Mussolini has remade them
> For tomorrow's war . . .

Their words had little effect. It stiffened a few backs, emboldening some of the prisoners and reminding them that their greatest quarrels were not with one another, but with their enemies. Convinced that the British were losing the war, they would point to the gulls that often flew above the huts, looking for any scraps the men dropped, some titbit or piece of bread that would keep their wings in flight. 'Soon it will be our Lightnings that will fly here, Englishmen. Our planes taking over your skies.'

Yet the majority did not feel that way, tired of Mussolini and all his imperial delusions. They wanted only to be fed again, to be left at peace even if it did mean they were being forced to suffer a little injustice. At a result of this, they felt only relief when the man from the Protecting Powers arrived in the camp – for all that they believed he had reached the wrong conclusions. He told the prisoners of war that there was no substance to the complaint they had made. The work they were doing was for peaceful reasons.

'So you'd better get back to work,' the gentleman from Switzerland concluded. 'There is no reason not to.'

5

STEPPING STONES

AN ITALIAN POW MEDITATES ON FIDELITY

Let us keep
(while we are parted)
chips of sandstone, dolomite within mind and heart
in case we weep
or falter in that dark
to which our love might succumb during long years alone.

Yet too we must retain sparks
from flint we clutch to strike off and ignite,
restore the flame that brought us here
these first nights,
spirit and flesh still burning till
the coming of first light.

It was a slip of the hand that caused it.

The young Domenico followed three of his friends in the area they knew as Roncac. It was a place where the Italian army carried out military exercises during the Great War, honing their skills for yet another assault on the Austrian forces with whom they had been in conflict for the previous year. Some of the debris of that warfare littered the field. Spent cartridges. Shattered shells. The imprint of soldiers' boots. At six years old, he trailed in the footsteps of the other, older, boys. Despite the fact that he was a cousin to one and brother to another they did not always have patience for him.

'Come on, Goti!' they yelled, using his childhood nickname. 'Get a move on!'

'Hurry up, you snail . . .!'

He tried his best, panting as he moved. As it was the end of August, there was still heat from the sun. Sweat trickled from his forehead. He felt impatient with himself – at his own lack of speed and the fact that he would never catch up with them, especially in terms of their years. He could only watch as they moved nimbly and quickly, shifting further and further away from him, racing across the field. In the distance, he could see one of the boys had a shell in his hand, one that had never been used. Again he felt a little envy, wishing he had their strength.

'Come on, Goti!' the cry echoed.

'Try and catch up with us!'

His fingers clenched, knowing he never could. Didn't they realise he was younger than them, didn't have their strength? He felt a strong surge of temper at the fact that even his own brother had forgotten that. They could be kinder to him, couldn't they? . . .

It was then it happened.

The scene that often replayed in his head even when he was older. It was hard to recall exactly how it occurred. A trip, perhaps, on a stone or incline. A foot that slid. Perhaps even a sudden realisation of the weight the boy was carrying in his hand. It made him flex his fingers, drop the unexploded bomb onto the field. There was the shock of an explosion. Mud and earth and human flesh thrown up together into that clear August sky . . .

Domenico Chiocchetti was around four years old when the armies of two of Europe's greatest nations wheeled and shifted round him.

When this occurred, it was, in its own way, as traumatic and overwhelming an event as the one that brought the Dolomites, the range of mountains that surrounded his childhood home, into existence. This time, however, it was not the work of Nature but of men. In turn, they were also its main victims. They were the ones that brought the Great War to these mountains, raining down bombs and artillery shells on each other. They were the ones who killed one another on mountain crests and valleys. They were the ones, too, who would create the next great tectonic movement in the lives of those who – like young Domenico – lived out their days in the shade of the Dolomites, shifting the national borders that surrounded them, turning them into citizens of a different country than the one into which they had been born.

On the morning of 23 May 1915, Domenico's parents were among those who probably attended morning Mass at the Church of San Vigilio in Moena. Among the other members of that Ladin-speaking community, they sat there in the pews while the priest told them of the events that were occurring outside the peaks – Sassolungo, Latemar, Rosengarten, Monzoni – that surrounded their quiet valley. Their nation, Austria-Hungary, was about to go to war with Italy, their close neighbour to the south. Greater beasts than any that haunted their folklore were on the move. Hostilities would begin the following day.

Some of the congregation would have sung more enthusi-astically than ever during Mass that morning, hoping that both God and the mountains would protect them from the armies mobilising on either side of them. '*Levavi oculos meos in montes, unde veniet auxilium mihi . . .*' they might have chorused together, hoping to gather courage from words the priest could have chosen for them to sing. 'I to the hills have raised mine eyes; from whence doth come mine aid . . .' They knew – as Orcadians must have known some quarter of a century later – that they were now in the front line of the conflict. There was the chance that the avalanche of war would engulf them. Some had feared the arrival of this moment since the previous year when one of Moena's parishioners, Caterina Pezze Batesta had scribbled an urgent, tearful entry for 24 June into her diary: 'While I am writing I cannot avoid crying! The Archduke Franz Ferdinand, crown prince, and his wife Duchess Sofia of Hohenberg have been murdered . . . I cried a lot and I am still crying.'

Even before that morning in May 1915, it had been clear there was good reason for Caterina's tears. A long period of stillness in the life of Moena was coming to an end. It was a period in which the people, no matter what language they spoke, identified themselves as Tirolese. This had changed with the coming of nationalism in the nineteenth century. The intellectuals and urban middle classes began to see themselves mainly as Italians; most of the rest of the population, especially the farmers, remained loyal to the Hapsburgs – their loyalty still to the man whose image was found on the coins the people of the Ladin community slipped into their offerings that day. Like their forbears since the middle of the previous century, each bore the profile of Emperor Franz Joseph, emperor of Austria and king of Hungary. On the throne since 1848 until his death in 1916, he had ruled over some 50 million subjects from diverse ethnic backgrounds. Of these, fewer than a quarter spoke German. Even within the boundaries of Austria itself, one in two were Slavs. They included Czechs, Slovaks, Ukrainians, Serbs, Croats, Slovenians and Poles, all nations which in the course of the twentieth century, would seek and gain independence for themselves, asserting their right to their own identity.

And then there were the other races, too small, perhaps, to ever gain a country of their own. They included, tragically for too many of that ethnic background, those of Jewish origin. Sigmund Freud spoke for them in 1918, declaring his sadness that Austria–

Hungary was 'no more . . . I do not want to live anywhere else.' In what was soon to become Italy, there were the Friulian people whose 500,000 or so speakers also lived in the north-east, near the Austrian and Slovenian border. And then too there were those, like Domenico, whose first language was the Ladin tongue. Too small and splintered a community ever to become a nation state, they did not even have the advantage of being a unified and cohesive group. They were neither Italian nor German; '*no taliegn, no todesc*' they said themselves. Among all those different people clamouring for their speech to be heard, their voices were both too hushed and too fractured to capture the attention of those around them.

There were reasons for this. Partly it was a matter of geography. The manner in which its speakers were separated by mountain crest and valley meant that there were six different versions of the Ladin tongue. It exists, for instance, in the canton of Grisons in Switzerland where since 1938, it has been seen as the nation's fourth national language. It lives on in the Friuli area, near Udine near Italy's south-eastern border. It survives in the Dolomites, in places like the Fassa valley where Domenico grew up and Ortisei in the Gardena valley where he lived and worked for a time. To complicate matters even more, there are local variants. In Cortina d'Ampezzo, it is the *soroio* that blazes in the noon-day sky; in Val Gardena, it is the *suredl*.

Yet there are many greater misunderstandings than those that can arise from the odd blurring of dialects, the shifts of vocabulary that might occur from one mountain range to another. There are those that take place when shots ring out, bringing an end to the lives of Archduke Franz Ferdinand and his wife Duchess Sofia in the streets of Sarajevo. The echo of the gunshots rang through the valleys in which the Ladin people made their homes long before the Italian army began to muster on the traditional borders, claiming the Alto Adige for its own. Not long after the archduke's assassin was arrested, it took some of its enlisted young men to

Galicia, a region of Austria–Hungary that now straddles Poland and Ukraine, to fight against the Russian troops in the autumn of 1914 and the spring of 1915. The legacy of that disastrous campaign can be found in the war memorial near St Vigilio's church in Moena. It contains a roll-call of names of those who died in the First and Second World Wars – for both the Hapsburg Empire in the first conflict and the Kingdom of Italy in the latter. Among them are those who were captured and deported to Siberia by Russian forces. Their experiences are recorded by Battista Chiocchetti* from Moena in his recollections of his time in exile in Omsk. He said that there were 1,600 imprisoned there in June 1915, 'out of which 6 were from Moena . . . Then I heard there are another 4 fellow villagers in other places.'

Yet if war was taking young men away from Moena, it was also advancing inexorably towards the township. Among those who spurred it on were men like Cesare Battisti, a whirlwind of political energy, demanding that Trento and its surrounding area should be made part of Italy. The first prominent activist to call for the abolition of Austria–Hungary, he was among those who convinced the more well-informed recruits to go to war.

'For Trento and Trieste! To get what was due to Italy. It was our land.'

Among those whose opinions were altered by men like Battisti and the trade union leader Filippo Corridoni was a young lantern-jawed journalist. He noted down the latter's words in the pages of the Socialist newspaper *Avanti*, writing of how only neutered men sought neutrality and that 'the Italian nation, once the old men in Rome have stopped delaying and called it to arms, shall not sheathe its sword before the Austrians have been hunted all the way across the Alps'.

It was one of the tragedies of the Ladin people that, on the morning of 23 May 1915, they were not only deafened by patriotic

---

* Not necessarily a relation of Domenico as the surname is common in Moena.

slogans but by the claims of two rival nationalisms, neither of which were their own. They were destined, too, to be among those trapped and ground between two opposing forces marching towards each other, each determined to claim the landscape they had decided they had inherited from their ancestors for their own.

When the invading armies arrived in the homeland of the Ladin people, their presence had a horrendous effect on the people there. In Cortina d'Ampezzo the remaining 669 fit and able males living within that town's borders lacked the ability to resist their Italian invaders in May 1915. Most of their men were away fighting for Austria–Hungary; those remaining were either very young or over 45 and had to fend for themselves without much support from their imperial masters. Cortina, a valuable crossroads at the centre of the Dolomites, was soon occupied by Italian troops.

The Ladin-speakers of Livinallongo suffered much more. Their town was fought over and bombarded throughout much of the war. A mountain of 2,262 metres in height nearby, the Col di Lana, was the scene of much bloody and brutal fighting. This was because the main highway through the area curled around an unusual outcrop of dark volcanic rock, in some ways more like the terrain Domenico might have seen travelling through the Scottish Highlands than his own native Dolomites. With light artillery on its twin summits, the Austrian troops could prevent anything much moving to the north or west of them. In July 1915, the assault began with 12 Italian infantry and 14 Alpini companies sacrificing their lives as they hurled themselves at their enemy's position on the top with disastrous and calamitous effect. It was a battle that mingled modern rifles and artillery with fierce and gruesome medieval weapons. Soldiers swung clubs and spiked maces. They aimed knuckle-dusters at their opponents, knocking them down the cliffs with their fists.

It was only in November that the Italians achieved any result. Having ringed the trenches near the two crests, they launched a fierce bombardment followed by a ferocious infantry assault. Following this, there was the most terrifying turn-around of troops. One instant, it might be the Italians on Col di Lana's crest, the next, the Austrians on the lower slopes. The only real results were the thousands of lives they had lost in attempting these attacks. It was a situation that deservedly earned it the nickname '*Col di Sangue*' or 'Blood Mountain' from the Italian troops who had lain down their lives in attempting to capture it.

The New Year brought new methods – both there and elsewhere, such as Castelletto in another part of the Dolomites. On 17 April 1916, the summit of Col di Lana was blasted and destroyed by a mine set by Italian sappers. Using hand-held drills and chisels, they had cut their way under the Austrian position, bringing them down in an explosion of rubble and dust that must have seemed as if the gateway to hell was opening, bringing down into its depths those who were standing on the summit, waiting, perhaps, for another desperate frontal attack. Instead, five tons of gelignite created an inferno of rock, ice and blood. It killed 150 soldiers with the blast, led to the imprisonment of almost the same number. It also left behind its own legacy to the landscape of the Dolomites – a huge crater which can even be seen today. For a little time afterwards, Italian feet stamped and marched upon its summit, yet the grip of their soles was to turn out to be tenuous and insecure. They never managed to capture Monte Sief, the neighbouring mountain. As a result, they had gained little military advantage from all the lives that had been lost in the winning of it. By October of the following year, Austrian boots swept away the foothold of the Italian forces in the aftermath of the Austro-Hungarian victory at Caporetto. The bloody pendulum had shifted back once again. Only the graveyard had proved to be a victor.

And so it was throughout the Dolomites as men from both armies set out to conquer their own particular Field of Miracles. Across the area, villages were evacuated of people; some never returning to the homes they had left. Communities were turned into barracks. Family homes were commandeered. The mountains that had shadowed them for centuries were turned into the most extraordinary backdrops for bloodshed and war. It was, after all, at up to 3,500 metres, the highest terrain at which a war had ever been fought, unmatched until the conflict between Chinese and Indian infantry in the early 1960s and the battles fought in Kashmir later. And by and large it was the double-headed eagle of the Austrian flag that flapped triumphantly from their eyries on their peaks. The Italian troops tried to cut their flagpoles from below, seeking to bring them down from the dizzy heights they occupied. It was a challenge in which both man's ingenuity and engineering ultimately failed. The defensive advantages of the Austro-Hungarian troops were too great for the courage of the Italians to overcome.*

So too was the most powerful foe that either army had to face in the Dolomites – the weather. The snow in itself killed many. Particularly in the first year of the war, it sometimes did this by revealing the silhouette of a soldier dressed in khaki clothes etched out against a white background. An enemy would raise his rifle; a trigger pulled; a man left dead. There were times when that same climate might protect them, stiffening fingers with frostbite, rendering them incapable of firing their guns. Soldiers, after all, might have to guard themselves against temperatures as low as −50°C in the depths of winter. Even summer sometimes brought sudden unexpected snowstorms. Water might freeze at night in August. Fingers could be forced to warm themselves on the nearest flame. On the tops of some of the higher peaks, there were quarters dug out from the ice that lay there all year around. Men lived in there, in that wintry wasteland, and were sometimes

---

* The Austro-Hungarians had difficulties too. It has been argued that nearly 900 porters working together in relay were required to give support and equipment to a garrison of 100 men on a mountain 3,000 metres or so above sea level.

driven mad by the constant bitter chill – a particular problem for the Austrian troops stationed on their heights. Sometimes there would be snow-blindness. It would send them lost and reeling across an unforgiving environment, one where one mistaken slip or stumble would send them skidding downwards to their deaths. And then there were the frequent avalanches. Sometimes they could be set off by the crack of gunfire. At other times, the snow could tumble down without warning, sweeping away men's lives, condemning them to a death where their scrambling, twisted bodies might be only discovered months later, uncovered by a thaw. On White Friday alone, 13 December 1916, around 10,000 soldiers died in this way.

Young Goti would only have been dimly aware of much of this. There was no doubt, however, that the slaughter had a great effect on Domenico's people in places like Moena in the Fassa valley. One of his neighbours, Caterina Pezze Batesta, confided her own fears about the state of humanity to the diary she wrote in most days. 'A punishment is needed for this war which sheds so much blood, so many tears, which turns men into wild beasts – yes, beasts, since days and months and years go by and there isn't the slightest sign of its end.'

It was probably a time, too, when dark tales were told in the *stua,* the room that was the centre of family existence. Panelled in Swiss wood with tiny windows that glinted in the morning sunlight, this was the only room to possess a stove. People would gather there in winter. The bench of Goti's father sat alongside it; its mere presence indicating that he was in charge of the household. He had probably sank down on it on the evening of 27 August 1916. When he discovered that one of his sons had been killed, he might have clung to the body of his youngest child, the sole survivor of that day the four boys had gone to look for souvenirs of the war.

'At least we've still got you, little one,' he could have said, 'At least we've still got you.'

That incident wasn't the only way the people of Moena suffered in the conflict. There had never been much to eat in the Fassa valley. Through a normal week, there was breakfast of barley, coffee and milk with rye bread or potatoes. At noon, there was polenta with cheese, milk or butter. The evening meal was likely to be boiled potatoes and milk soup. Only on Sunday might there be a little pork, mingled with barley. By 1918, however, there was less even than that.

Many men had been killed in the conflict, their blood like its own pink thread in the red rock of the Dolomites. There were some who still had to make their way home, lost in the chaos that followed the conflict. People had withdrawn into themselves, shocked and shaken by the years of war. Fields were left unploughed, harvests ungathered, the population retreating in a different way from all the armies that once wheeled and stirred around them, hiding from the grim and overwhelming realities of their lives.

The war certainly put an end to the tourist industry that the people of areas like the Fassa valley had already began to depend on by the beginning of the First World War. Tales of the area's natural beauty had begun to draw the rich and prosperous from throughout the continent of Europe by the end of the nineteenth century. At first, there were the geologists. They followed in the wake of Déodat de Dolomieu, the scholar who gave the Dolomites their name. He was the individual who chipped off a small piece of rock to discover within the dual salts of calcium and magnesium that made the rock flush a bright shade of pink when the evening sun glinted on it.

After the geologists there came the naturalists to gape at the wonder of its mountains, the beauty of its forests and the variety of its wildlife. There were even some who did more than this, their footsteps stepping tentatively on the precipitous slopes, cliffs and crevasses of the mountain range, trying to make their way to their summits. To help them do this, they relied on the expertise of those whose knowledge of these mountains had been bred into them for generations. They were the hunters, taught by their fathers to scan the slopes for the presence of chamois, the deer-like animals that grazed and concealed themselves near the crest.

There were also the shepherds, skilled at spotting each small patch of grazing to be found among its hills. Their eyes could sense the dangers in each tumble of stone or ice sheet, knowing precisely where to place their feet in order to make each step safe and secure. Their ears were sharp, tuning into every sound that might tell them an avalanche was about to speed down upon them and their flocks. It was through all this they acquired their mastery of this geography, one that enabled them to guide the early mountaineers towards the peaks they so desperately and inexplicably wished to conquer.

All this had brought the Ladin people money. It even provided work in the hotels that were built throughout the Dolomites at that time, giving geologists, naturalists, mountaineers and others a bed where they could sleep for the night. They would craft toys, too, to sell to their visitors, painted in the bright blue shade of *Fassanerblau*, decorated with the tiny illustrations of birds and flowers that were the region's trademark.

Yet there were times in the war years when toys like that gathered dust in people's houses. There were no visitors in the hotels to buy. There were no mountaineers willing to brave the barbed wire that remained on their mountainsides or to run the risk of stepping on an artillery shell embedded in the snow like the one that had killed Domenico's playmates. To tourists, the Dolomites seemed a stark, harsh and jagged geography where one might discover corpses rotting among mountain flowers, the chamois grazing nearby. Its only geology was fear, the constant threat of discovering the black and desiccated shape of death on a slope or peak. There was no possibility of the fit and healthy Ladin men going to the towns or cities to sell their gifts or practise their trade. Few there had money; the ones that did kept their fists tightly clenched, refusing to allow a coin to slip. There would be another time for city churches to be restored, another age to buy a brightly painted carving.

The words of the priest reverberated in these troubled times:

Da, Domine, propitius pacem in diebus nostris, ut, ope miseri-cordiae tuae adiuti, et a peccato simus semper liberi et ab omni perturbatione securi. Per Christum Dominum nostrum. Amen.

Graciously give peace, O Lord, in our days, that, being assisted by help of Thy mercy, we may ever be free from sin and safe from all disturbance. Through Christ our Lord. Amen.

ॐ

In the South Tyrol Museum of Archaeology in the city variously known as either Bolzano or Bozen, I encounter the dead-eyed gaze of a gentleman called Ötzi. He has probably the least healthy complexion of anyone I have ever met. His lean and hungry-looking face has a green, copper-like shade. He also has his left arm bent across his naked chest, as if he feels defensive, protecting himself from the eyes of others intruding into his privacy at all times. This is probably because, ever since he was dragged out into the light, he is aware he stirs the curiosity of onlookers. He is, in fact, a well-preserved natural mummy of a man from about 3300 BC, discovered in September 1991 in the Schnalstal glacier in the Ötztal Alps, near Hauslabjoch on the border between Austria and Italy. Europe's oldest natural human mummy, he has been preserved by ice rather than the peat which has performed that task elsewhere in our continent.

For all that snow and ice may have brought about his death, violence also played a part in it. Scientists analysing his equipment found there were traces of the DNA of others on it. One man's blood was on his knife; that of two others were on an arrowhead in his possession. There was also a wound caused by an arrowhead piercing his shoulder, his body twisting and turning in agony as he tried to remove it. He also received, too, a blow on his head, perhaps inflicted by someone throwing a rock in his direction. Aside from the suffering that would have marked his life, there was no doubt that human brutality brought a swift and sudden end to it – pattern that was to mark these mountains for centuries.

Even today, there are signs of that violent inheritance evident in the area. The turrets of a clutch of castles are to be found around Bolzano. They include Castle Maretsch, Castle Sigmundskron and Runkelstein Castle, the last-named built back in the thirteenth century and subjected to a number of sieges since. Among the faces to be seen at various sites throughout the region is that of Andreas Hofer, a Tyrolean innkeeper who led an army of his fellow countrymen against Napoleon's forces at the beginning of the nineteenth century, trying to halt the French emperor's plans to put the area under Bavarian control. He was shot by a firing squad. His dark, hairy-chinned features have achieved a kind of immortality, found on plates, posters, and even – perhaps – the occasional old-fashioned shaving mug found in the antique shops in Bolzano, the Che Guevara of his age. In his opposition to the French, he created a breed of Tyrolean patriots, uniting German, Italian and Ladin speakers with a sense of shared identity.

The course of the nineteenth century brought an end to much of that – many of the German and Italian-speakers beginning to gain a sense of their own identity, one that was generated largely by the distinctive tongue they had in common. This was intensified in the closing years of the First World War which brought another time of turbulence for the people of Moena and other towns and villages in the Ladin homeland. The change was summed up by Caterina Pezze Batesta from Domenico's home town in her little diary with the words, 'November 9, 1918. We have become Italians!!'

Whether they noted its arrival with a brace of exclamation marks or not, it was a transformation that was not without a great deal of discomfort for many of the area's inhabitants. They had long grown used to Austrian ways. The flag of the South Tyrol flapped above their municipal buildings, the 'double eagle' displayed on their walls. The grey and whiskered features of Emperor Franz Josef had smiled benignly on them from his portrait on the town hall walls for more than a few decades.

There was a comfort in that familiarity; the Ladin people were treated the same as any of Franz Josef's multitude of subjects, part of a large multi-ethnic state.

Many had learned to have faith in all of that, even the postage stamp with the Emperor's image they fixed in the corner of letters sent out to the fathers and husbands who spent much of the year working away from home. They had learned to trust the solidity and dependability of these long and twisting roads the emperor had provided them with in the last years of the nineteenth century, a prodigious achievement as they coiled around each precipitous slope. They had learned, too, to rely on their schools, the reading, writing and arithmetic they had provided for their children. Sometimes they would even talk disparagingly about the schools over the border, in the south.

'They're not the same down there. Not so many can read or write ...'

But now they had to learn to live in 'Italy', among the people that some of them had half-despised and feared. They may have been worried that revenge might be taken on them because when Ladin men had fought in the Austro-Hungarian army their knowledge of their mountain surroundings had been a source of strength for Italy's foes. They might have been afraid that the people of their new nation would be aware that some of them wished to remain part of Austria or to be recognised as their own distinctive ethnic group; the phrase 'no taliegn, no todesc' was created around this time. As a result, they felt smaller and more vulnerable than they had ever done before, cursing the fact that they were caught between two great nations without any real voice or choice of their own.

Yet in the beginning, many felt it might all be a simple, easy change for them. The Italian language was not unknown to them. In fact, it was considered the first language of culture and recognised by their former Hapsburg Empire as the official tongue for the whole of the Trentino area. (They also spoke German, seen as 'the language of bread'.) They could easily find their way across the stepping stones between the two cultures. Neither tongue was a barrier to them.

It was helped by the fact that in general the Italians seemed well disposed to them, introducing only a few small changes to their lives. In their towns and villages, new postage stamps with the words '*Poste Italiane*' were sold over the counters of the local post office. The features of their new monarch, King Victor Emmanuel III, with his bristling black moustache looked down on the customers and postal clerks. Occasionally they would whisper to one another about how unimpressive he was compared to old Franz Josef with his grey hair thick upon his upper lip. No real king at all.

'They say he's only five feet tall . . .' young Goti might hear them mutter.

'Don't worry . . . We'll soon get used to it,' they smiled.

They both treasured and nurtured that hope, drawing strength from it when they felt their new Italian government had misunderstood the nature of the people they governed. The regime failed to realise that in places like the Fassa valley people spoke Italian regularly and fluently, as unlike much of the country to their south, basic schooling had existed in the South Tyrol since the seventeenth century. This led to situations like the arrival of Italian soldiers in the Dolomites, armed with basic spelling books to assist the citizens with the difficulties of their new tongue. As they handed them to the locals, they were surprised by the bemusement with which their gifts were received, the mountain-men barely able to suppress their laughter.

Despite this, the Ladin people looked forward to the steady

return of visitors intent on exploring the mountains and rocks, flora and wildlife. It was probably then that Goti's parents began to talk tentatively of opening a small hotel for tourists when peace became more secure and the world more prosperous. It was something they managed to do a number of years later, the young man helping them in the task of welcoming visitors to their home.

Yet all this was undermined by a bewildering progression of events. There was a local economic crisis, later deepened by the depression of 1929. It was influenced by the loss of commercial ties on which they had long depended, those with the rest of the Tyrol and Austria as a whole, the devaluation of the Italian currency, loss of jobs, even the abolition of laws and customs which had regulated the use of forests and fields. Like much of Europe, their new nation of Italy was troubled by political violence. Slogans daubed in red paint appeared on walls, extolling the virtues of the new men in Russia: Lenin and the Bolsheviks. There were fights between strikers and the police. Arson, sabotage, theft and murder – all the work of moments when huge crowds lost control and attacked those with whom they came into contact. The worst of these events took place in regions like Piedmont, Lombardy, Tuscany, Emilia-Romagna, once exotic and strange to the people of the Fassa valley but which now appeared to be moving closer and closer to their homes. They trembled at the thought of that turmoil in their midst.

So they looked around for reassurance, evidence that little had altered. They saw this in the 'double eagles' that still adorned many of the public buildings in their localities. The signposts hadn't changed; the word 'Bozen' still pointed the way to the town their new masters referred to as 'Bolzano'. In its city hall, the old Austrian elite were still in control of the council. The familiar figure of Julius Perathoner still survived as mayor.

And then in 1920 there arose a new group among their neighbours to the south – one that, according to their young and energetic leader, was the only force that could save their country,

The Northern Lights in the Northern Isles (Ivan Hawick)

The Barriers at a time of war – painting by Ian Macinnes
(Alastair and Anne Cormack)

The Italian 'Olympic' Prize-winners in July 1944 (James W. Sinclair)

Lining up for a shot – the prisoners at the billiard table (James W. Sinclair)

The Concrete Bowling Alley (James W. Sinclair)

Trumpeting the Arrival of St George (James W. Sinclair)

Gathering round St George (James W. Sinclair)

Domenico restoring the crest of Moena in 1960 (Orkney Library Archives)

The most well-known photograph of the Chapel, showing 24 of the men who were involved in its creation. They include Domenico Chiocchetti at the far left; Palumbi is the dark figure with the moustache standing at the pillar. Photograph by James W. Sinclair (Orkney Library Archives)

A view of St Mary's and the Barriers (Tom Muir)

The weathered Wayside Shrine, bearing up to the onslaught of wind and wave (Tim Wright)

The bell-tower of the Chapel (Tom Muir)

The Chapel in its setting on a pleasant summer's day (Tom Muir)

St George triumphant against the dragon (Tim Wright)

The man of constant sorrow; the suffering head of Christ (Tim Wright)

Before its metamorphosis – the Nissen hut (Tom Muir)

After the metamorphosis – an interior shot (Tom Muir)

The chancel of the Chapel, where Palumbi and Chiocchetti performed their first act of transformation (Tom Muir)

Even the bully beef tins provide a source of light; the intricate ironwork bears a message of faith (Tom Muir)

Chiocchetti's masterpiece – the Madonna and Child (Tom Muir)

One of the many panels in the Chapel nave, the creations of both Pennisi (from the Burray camp) and Chiocchetti (Tom Muir)

Chiocchetti's final creation – the holy water stoup; its base fashioned from a large spring found in one of the workshops (Tom Muir)

The longing for home – the town-crest of Moena within a cherub's clasp
(Tim Wright)

St Matthew and St Mark (Tim Wright)

The longing for home 2 – the dove in exile (Tim Wright)

St Luke and St John (Tim Wright)

Domenico and Maria enjoying the spring sunshine (John Muir)

Domenico with John Muir of the
Italian Chapel Preservation Committee
in his home in Moena in later life
(John Muir)

Domenico's daughter, Letizia, receiving
the title of Honorary President of the
Chapel Preservation Committee from
John Muir (John Muir)

'The place of nettles': Ortisei, where Domenico trained as an artist
(Maria Robertson)

The Victory Gate, Bolzano, with its solemn warning to the German population of the town (Maggie Priest)

'I to the hills …': A view of the Dolomites (Andrew Robertson)

uniting them against the menace of Bolshevism. They did this with clubs and grenades, rifles and guns that were sometimes even supplied to them by the local police force or army barracks. When they punished an opponent, they performed the act of forcing them to swallow castor oil, purging them of political sin. They began arriving in the local towns of Auer and Salorno in February 1921, tearing down the 'double eagles' from wherever they could find them. Shortly after that, the sign for 'Bozen' was torn down too.

Even among the Ladin population, there were some who continued to love their new nation of Italy, but it became increasingly difficult to do this after events like the one that took place on 24 April 1921 when the Blackshirts arrived in Bolzano. On that sunlit day in spring, many of the townspeople were gathered in their traditional costumes for the *Trachtenumzug*, a ceremonial procession that marked the opening of the town fair. Cowbells rang as they dangled from the yokes sitting on the shoulders of young men. Girls with long, colourful dresses waved to the crowds whose hands rang with loud applause.

There had been some hints that trouble might come. Over the border in Innsbruck in Austria, a plebiscite was taking place, one that voted overwhelmingly for the unification of North and South Tyrol and there were suggestions that the procession was deliberately timed to coincide with it. The German Association had asked for protection to be given to the event. Nothing, however, could have prepared them for what was to follow. A group of 280 Fascists arrived by train in the town to join 120 others who had already gathered there. They came equipped to make their own contribution to the festivities, swinging clubs, firing pistols and even throwing hand grenades into the crowd. In the melee, 50 South Tyroleans were injured. One man, the teacher Franz Innerhofer, was shot while protecting a child. It was at this stage soldiers intervened, seeking to protect the Fascists as they made their way back to the train.

There was, understandably, a great sense of outrage about all that had occurred. Much of it came from the German speakers on both sides of the Austro-Italian border. However, it did not come exclusively from a northerly direction. It was, perhaps, at that time that the name of Benito Mussolini first reached young Domenico's ears. 'If the Germans on both sides of the Brenner don't toe the line,' he pronounced, 'then the Fascists will teach them a thing or two about obedience.' He continued to speak, threatening and cajoling as his neck strained from the high collar he often wore at these times. The giant fist clumped the wooden boards again. 'If the Germans have to be beaten and stomped to bring them to reason, then so be it, we're ready. A lot of Italians have been trained in this business.'

There were reminders of this for months to come. When two men were arrested for their part in Franz Innerhofer's death, Mussolini threatened to arrive in the town at the head of 2,000 Fascists to force their release. It was a warning that laid the basis for much that was to follow. It wasn't long before the Fascists with all their earthly forces occupied the City Hall in Bolzano, taking over the building and then the town council in October. Soon after, their leader marched on Rome*, occupying the Piazza Venezia in the Eternal City. Dressed occasionally in a Blackshirt uniform, young Goti learned to repeat the slogans his teacher taught him to proclaim. '*Duce! Duce! Duce! We are yours to the end*,' he might declare, for all that he was put off by the mockery of his older brothers. There was also the Fascist anthem, '*Giovinezza*' which his teacher used to rehearse endlessly in class; its chorus like a hymn upon his classmates' lips.

> *Giovinezza, Giovinezza,*
> *Primavera di belleza . . .*
>
> Youth, youth,
> Spring of beauty . . .

---

* Contrary to legend, Mussolini actually travelled to the capital by train.

He read, too, the words of the Fascist South Tyrolean newspaper when it pronounced: 'This region must become Italian, and its inhabitants must become Italians, so that everything here is Italian and brings to mind only Italy.'

There were some who muttered about this. After all, like Domenico, many of the Ladin speakers' second language was German, which they had learned since their early years at school. Among the complainers was Domenico's future father-in-law, Frederico Felicetti. As a former captain of the Standschützen, he would growl in the direction of any young person who showed enthusiasm for the new regime. Describing the Italians as '*canalin*', dogs, he would declare, '*Te n'ai dat int en lecion.* They've booted you up the arse.'

If Goti ever heard him speak like that, he might have regarded his words as the ramblings of an old and cynical man, unworthy of taking seriously. It was in the new nation that Goti grew up, finding his own way of skirting round the chasms and gulfs that might exist in his landscape. He did this first when tourists began to return to the region, reassured by a few years of peace and the iron presence of Il Duce in Rome.

Once again the people of Moena could sing the Ladin words of Psalm 121 quietly under their breath: '*Gio oute i eies envers i monc, da olà me vegniràl aiut?* I to the hills will lift mine eyes; from whence doth come mine aid?' There was much aid to be obtained from the hills. Visitors were beginning to step out on the slopes of the Dolomites, drawn there once again by their beauty and deep snow. The carved toys and goods the people of the region were famous for were no longer accumulating on the shelves of the local shops but being sold over their counters. Hotels and guest houses were filling up again after a time of uncertainty. *Fassanerblau* was starting once more to shade the sky. Their new currency, the lire, was going from hand to hand. With all that, it was getting easier to live with the shadows cast upon their lives by the Blackshirts and their desire to make all those who lived within their borders 'good Italians'.

Young Goti discovered his own freedom in music and art. The latter was abundant in his home town. Frescoes of St Christopher and St Ursula were painted on the walls of many of the buildings throughout the Fassa valley, their warmth and colours sheltering him as he walked through its streets in midwinter, protecting him from being dispirited too much by snow and cold wind. They were particularly entwined in the Church of San Vigilio which his family attended. As he prayed, he would look up at the work of the town's most famous painter, Valentino Roviso. He had been a student of Tiepolo in Venice, learning from the work of a great artist whose vast luminous canvases were seen throughout Europe. When Goti contemplated Roviso's skills with a brush, he felt something akin to envy. Perhaps the day might come when he would be able to create his own memorial to God's glory, his own witness to peace in the world. It was something which most men said they wanted, yet few ever stretched out a finger to achieve.

There was, too, another kind of freedom – the one he obtained through being in the company of older men like Frederico Felicetti. As they played cards together, the youngster might have coaxed the older man into telling a few stories of the war he had experienced, creating a shiver through his body that was much greater than any of those generated by the wind and cold outside. 'Awful. Awful,' Frederico might say, before altering the subject. There were times, too, when Domenico would catch himself taking a look at Frederico's pretty dark-haired daughter, Maria, some six years younger than him, watching the swirl of her dress, the quiet grace with which she held herself. There were so many ways in which her looks were more unsettling than any of the wonderful paintings he saw in the church.

But there was another distraction, the sense that he had to follow in the tracks of thousands of his fellow townsmen – leaving the valley where he had been born and brought up. Knowing that his future lay in his skills in art, he headed to the place that had been called Ortisei on the maps he had been shown in the schoolroom but others knew as St Ulrich or Urtijei. There were talents he could learn there, and he was fortunate enough to have the opportunity of being taught by Viktor Pitscheider, a teacher of sacred art renowned throughout the region. He made his way towards the Val Gardena, knowing that there were many of his fellow Ladin speakers there. He felt at ease with these people. In the expressions of his native tongue, there was all the warm familiarity of an older world ...

᠅

Il Duce was doing his best to change the reality of the world elsewhere.

In Bolzano, he decided to erect a monument in the exact spot near the Talfer Bridge where the former German-speaking council had began to build their own memorial to the Austrian Kaiserjaeger troops who had fallen during World War One. Called the Victory Monument, it was inaugurated in July 1928 by King Victor Emmanuel III and a group of Fascist dignitaries. The 19-metre-wide monolith is still there today, recalling the lives lost by Italian soldiers in the First World War while fighting the sons and fathers of many of those who lived nearby, soldiers in the service of the Austro-Hungarian Empire. On its marble columns, Fascist symbols such as axe blades are carved. Facing the city, there is a sculpture of Vittoria Sagittaria, a semi-clad huntress firing an arrow north towards those in Austria who wish this part of their former kingdom to be restored. Below it, a Latin inscription is chiseled in stone.

HIC PATRIAE FINES SISTE SIGNA HINC CETEROS EXCOLUIMUS LINGUA LEGIBUS ARTIBUS.

Here are the borders of the fatherland. Put down your weapons. From here, we civilised the rest of the world in language, laws and arts.

There is little doubt what most of Bolzano's German-speaking inhabitants thought of all this back in 1928. Each word and note of condescension cut into them like a wound; each of the stones within the column grinding them down like a huge weight upon their backs. They were aware that Mussolini and his Fascists intended all this as an insult against them, reinforcing the lesson some of them had even learned in school: that they did not quite belong in this new nation the mapmakers had drawn out for them. Over the following years there were more and more reminders of this. Italian speakers were brought in from all over the north of the country, from Veneto, Belluno, Vicenza, Verona and other regions and cities, to settle in Bolzano, transforming it into an industrial city. In 1936, there were hardly any native Italian speakers. By 1943, some 7,000 had arrived. By 1947, a further 12,000 had come. With them, too, a new and 'Roman' city had also transformed the look of much of the city's outskirts. Walk between the Victory Monument and the formerly outlying district of Gries today and you feel much as Pinocchio must have felt as he stepped through a dark forest, fearful of all the shadows that have been cast around him by great trees. In this case, the tree trunks are heavy, faceless blocks, examples of what has been termed 'rational architecture', the foundation stones of the new and powerful empire Mussolini planned to build. With their cold, damp quarters, and bereft of places where the occupants can meet or socialise, it is the creation of a man who rarely laughed, except when scorning or trying to impress others.

Domenico Chiocchetti is a very different kind of man. He spends much of his time in churches in the 'place of nettles', Urtijei, taking note, for instance, of all the artwork found in the great parish church there. He helps Viktor Pitscheider restore and renew all the sculptures and paintings on display within its walls. It is sometimes the work of such men as Franz Xaver Kirchebner, Josef Moroder-Lusenburg and Josef Mersa, names that make him pause and wonder when he replenishes and restores the paint on some of their artistic creations. When he has completed his years of apprenticeship, he sets out into the world, going to larger towns and cities like Belluno or Bolzano in the company of his friend Vigillio Sommariva. They work together on its great and magnificent churches. There is work to be found in places like that; money that can ring in his empty pockets, acts of faith and artistry he can perform.

Even his national service adds to his skills. He goes to Mantua where he sees the work of Andrea Mantegna, the great Renaissance artist, on display. Examining a series of frescoes based on the life of St James, which would be largely destroyed in the Second World War, the young man is reminded of the brutality of the Roman state which Mussolini is attempting to recreate. In one, St James is being led to his death through a Roman arch by a group of legionaries, his fingers stretching out to bless a penitent as he goes. This strange ambiguity is found time and time again in Mantegna's paintings, the artist celebrating Rome while at the same time revealing that its very foundations are based on conquest and brutality, much like Il Duce's own.

And so Domenico learns from all this art. He adds light and texture to the creations of others, freshening them for the faithful who crowd into the churches to worship and pray. They look up to see old images become as bright and gleaming as they had been when they were first set in place in the building's walls. He hears them murmur – both in German and Italian – words in praise of the miracles he has done.

This is his power, not like that of Mussolini with his ability to command men, set blocks of stone in position. It is his way, too, of standing apart from the disputes of these men who might sometimes stand below him as he works away on the ceiling of some fine church. He is a Ladin, after all, not wholly Italian. The quarrels of the two races who surround him and dominate his life are not a major part of his existence. He wants only to stand at some distance from them when they fight.

Yet even he cannot help but become aware of the tensions and disagreements that exist between the two great cultures of his region. They impinge on him even in his isolation. Something evil is being let loose. The monsters are emerging from their places in the mountain. He can hear the sound of their jackboots pounding the streets below.

He is especially aware of it every time he puts on his national service uniform, conscious that he is being garbed and clothed for a war that is not of his choosing. He is not even certain who he is going to be fighting against. One moment, it looks as if it might be Germany, a battle which many of those who speak that language seem to be longing for, looking, like those in Austria, for *Anschluss* or 'political union' with that state. The next, it might be Great Britain or France, who seem to be plotting against Italy's rightful desire to obtain an empire of their own.

Over the last while, the latter has become more likely. Domenico heard, after all, the words Mussolini spoke at the end of the military manoeuvres that took place in Bolzano in 1935. His strength and energy was on display then, his voice strong and forceful as it echoed across a field full of uniformed soldiers. He spoke of the sanctions that had been placed on the country after their invasion of Abyssinia, declaring that normally after their grand parade, they would have been

let free from duty, but this year this is not going to happen. By September, 200,000 more men will be joining your platoons to bring the levels of soldiers in the army to the suggested number of 1 million men. The world must know once more that until people stop speaking in an absurd and provoking way about sanctions, we will not cut our army by one single foot soldier, one single sailor or horse soldier, but we will take instead our number of soldiers to the maximum number possible nationally. Soldiers, airmen, seamen, and black shirts too, your deeds of the last few days but especially the very

high morale that gives you strength, give us the certainty
that if tomorrow our country will call you to defend us and
to perform your duty, you shall do it with enthusiasm, with
courage, with determination to the very last moment. Soldiers,
let us salute the king! Hail to the King!

It was on this afternoon that it probably occurred to Domenico
for the first time that he might be going to war, to fight in the
Field of Miracles for the bright and futile causes of others.

ɔ

As I head across the Waltherplatz in Bolzano for ten o'clock Mass
at the Cathedral of Our Lady of the Assumption, the town's most
important church, I wonder if I follow in Domenico's footsteps.
Along with me are a large number of elderly German-speaking
men and women. Some of them might even have been youngsters
in 1939, the time when Mussolini's Italy and Hitler's Germany
finally agreed to swap citizens across their national borders. This
was an exchange that never fully took place because the full
horrors of war intervened to prevent the movement, though
a number of German and Ladin speakers went to live in the
territories of the Reich, while others not in favour were interned
in Italy.

A handful arrive late, slipping into the pews after the ceremony
has begun. Their heads are crouched, half-apologetically, as the
priest stands before them, dressed in green vestments, his glasses
glinting in the thin light of the church. Its windows are, after all,
shrouded by billboards and scaffolding due to the fact that the
building is being renovated, restoring its brightly painted roof, the
frescoes on its outside walls. I think to myself that this is similar
work to that performed by Domenico, his brush restoring health
to pale, washed-out cheeks, a spark to their eyes.

As someone who comes from a Presbyterian background who
has only a bare smattering of German, much of the ceremony

is incomprehensible to me. An elderly woman with grey hair wrapped in a dark headscarf reads from a hymn book as she leads the singing of '*Wer intern Schetz der Hochstein steth . . .*' Feeling both ignorant and ill at ease, I do not bother trying even to mouth the words, knowing that I did so I would only perform a passable impersonation of an English politician moving his lips in rhythm with the sounds he imagines hearing at the Welsh *Eisteddfod*. No force in the world is strong enough to make me look quite as ridiculous as that. Instead, I stand still and wait for the ordeal to be over.

And then comes a moment that is more familiar. A sign beside the priest declares the next hymn to be sung. I leaf through the book to find Hymn 752, recognising the words as those of Psalm 121. '*Ich hebe mein Augen auf zan Bergen, Wohr Kommt mir Hilfe?*' These are words familiar to me from childhood in both Gaelic and English. 'I to the hills will lift mine eyes; from whence doth come mine aid?' My father used to sing these words as, psalmody in hand, he stood before the congregation in Cross Church of Scotland in the Isle of Lewis – a favourite verse but one that seemed almost inappropriate in that flat, low-lying island.

It seems much more fitting here. Outside Bolzano, there are indeed hills to which men lift their eyes. The strange, otherworldly shapes of the Dolomites dominate the city, their pinnacles and peaks looking like a haggle of old woman gazing downwards on the streets below. It is easy to imagine them concealing dark, primeval forces about to sweep down and bring death and destruction to that land. It is easy, too, to picture Domenico, praying for God and all his angels to protect them. He had seen and heard enough of all that war could do to men: the stories of White Friday, 13 December 1916, when 10,000 soldiers died; *Col di Sangue*, Blood Mountain; the destruction of Livinallongo. He wanted no more of that to happen, he decided, mouthing the prayer he had learned in childhood.

Da, Domine, propitius pacem in diebus nostris, ut, ope misericordiae tuae adiuti, et a peccato simus semper liberi et ab omni perturbatione securi. Per Christum Dominum nostrum. Amen.

A moment after these words had died on his lips, he rose to his feet. In his mind, once again, was the image of what had occurred on 27 August 1916. The six-year-old frustrated at his inability to catch the older boys. Watching them moving away from him while his tired legs struggled to keep up. His eyes blinking back tears, finding it impossible to respond when they shouted.

'Come on, Goti! Get a move on!'

'Hurry up, you snail!'

Until that blast halted their progress.

Until that slip of the hand took away their lives.

6

CHANNELS

ST CATHERINE'S TEARS

St Catherine who sought to catalogue men's tears
never considered these ones, cast across the dark
of Northern skies, like sparks struck off an anvil.
They did not fill men's hearts with grief but wonder. They spilled
over constellations, kindling awe in those who saw each gleam
as proof light was present and had accompanied
them on their voyage across waters, towards islands
where for too long they'd felt that wind and rain
imprisoned them, that even sea and squall could not storm walls
holding them in the grip of such humiliation, pain.

And so in all these tears she listed, those of life or death,
love or lust, guilt or penance, did she ever glimpse or notice
that cosmic dance spiralling across Siena's streets or those of Florence?
Did she ever glance at meteors or pulsars, stellar rings and jets
thronging the heavens above Orkney, the aurora borealis
that baffles these observers, reminding them
their sorrow's dwarfed by this display,
that even the grief of mothers who have lost their child in war
can be healed for an instant by those tears that fleck the darkness,
sweeping up their sorrow with each bright incoming wave?

It was the first time he had really seen Orcadians.

Of course, it was true that there were those working alongside who came from Orkney, but they barely even registered on his eyeline, blending into the melee of mud, machines and other men working for Balfour Beatty on the site, their presence obscured by rain. These ones were different. There was no sign of dirt in their fingernails or engrained on their fingers. They had smooth skin, unbruised and uncut by hammer-blow or slip of chisel. Their shoes and clothes were pressed and clean. Domenico watched them as they entered the office of the new camp commander, Major Buckland, seeing the men as reminders of the world as it had been before the war, a place where normal, peaceful people existed.

It was the portly old gentleman with a white moustache and a walking stick who did most of the talking while they were in there. Major Buckland translated his every word. On occasion, he did this clumsily, grasping for the right expression, faltering as it failed to come to his lips. His blue eyes held steady. They seemed to gather everyone who was in the room into his gaze, a remarkable feat for someone who was impressive in neither stature nor physique, though it might have been caused by the fact, that, in his early fifties, Tom Buckland was older than the rest of the soldiers in the room.

The old gentleman was talking about the people of the islands to the south, how they were sometimes cut off for weeks in the winter, unable to get provisions for themselves or their homes. 'You've seen the waves lash here, haven't you? Imagine what that does to a small boat in winter. Sometimes in summer too. It's terrifying. Terrifying. Especially for these poor folks who have to go to Kirkwall to attend hospital. Life and death situations. Made all the worse by the waves.'

He paused, waiting for his words to be transformed by Major Buckland. As he did so, he looked at the Italian soldiers intensely, as if he were trying to dredge up compassion from somewhere behind the rustic uniforms they wore, targeting them with his speech. 'Think of a woman suffering complications in childbirth, how that short sea voyage adds to her misery . . .'

Again, the pause, the look that searched for some signs that the men were giving consideration to his words. The Italians tried not to be drawn in by it, swayed by the musicality of his accent, so different from many others they had heard since arriving in the country. Most of the time their guards and the site workers used harsh words edged by curses. 'There are other ways this causeway might help us. It isn't that long ago – I remember it all too well – when a young girl with the surname of Robson and two men were drowned in that channel here. She was only 16. The family haven't got over it. Never . . .'

'People have been killed since they started building the Barriers . . .' Petrucci pointed out.

'*Si*,' Primavera nodded. They had heard tales about how these deaths happened. On one occasion, there had been a fault in the cableway across Kirk Sound from Lamb Holm to St Mary's. It had brought the skip down into the water with a crash. Unable to escape the strength of the tide, three of the men who were in it drowned. There had been the time, too, when they had lost control of a home-made raft bringing some 30 men from a boat to the shore. Terrified by the force of a current, three dived into the sea. Only one was ever fished out again. Apart from these, there were probably other occasions they had never heard about when men working on the Barriers were killed.

'There's no doubt that these things happened and that it's awful when it does. But at the end of the day, this causeway will save the lives of people . . .'

'*Si*.' Primavera spat. 'The lives, perhaps, of British sailors. The lives of men on ships like the great *Royal Oak* who will go out and kill our people: Italian seamen.'

'No. No. No. That's not how I see it,' the old man smiled. 'My name is Flett. My people have been born and brought up here for many years. I hope they will continue to be here for many years to come. When all the Royal Navy ships have long gone. When those who work here will be gone.' He dipped a thumb into his waistcoat pocket, playing with the little gold chain that looped and trailed outside. 'A lifetime,' he said, looking directly at Primavera. 'I want to protect all those who will spend all their lives here and make this a good place to live. That's especially the case when it's women, children, bambinos. Those innocent of this war. They need this causeway to protect their lives, to enable others to reach them in winter. I'm asking you to help us in this. Wouldn't you want people to do this for your community, your small villages and towns? Don't you have roads that allow your people to travel freely? Don't you think these people should have the same?'

The Italians could not help considering what the old man was saying. Domenico thought of the way men like Frederico Felicetti had talked about how life had been in towns like Moena before Franz Josef had ordered roads to be built across the length and breadth of his kingdom. 'It was a hard life then,' he had said, 'Months when we couldn't shift, when we were cut off by snow. I tell you, young people today couldn't stand it.'

His daughter Maria had smiled when he spoke like this, as if they were words she had heard a thousand times before. She was older by this time, talking about going away to Rome to find work. Domenico had felt a twinge of sadness every time he heard this. He would miss her life and laughter about the *stua,* always in the background when the men were playing cards.

In the office of Major Buckland, the old man continued: 'You have to do it anyway, whether you like it or not. Your Swiss friends have told you that. And I can understand why you might not want to. I would hate having to work away on the other side of the world, alongside people you fought against before, who tried to kill you and you tried to kill. I would hate that. But you might as well live with it and try your best to bring some good out of evil.

The causeway will be here when you're gone. It'll be here when I'm gone. And it'll be bringing life and peace and hope to the people in these islands. Think of that ...'

Primavera continued to spit when they left the office, his big feet splashing through the mud and puddles as he made his way across the site towards Domenico. In a few moments he had spluttered out a condensed version of the conversation – one that ended with the words, 'Causeway? Causeway? What's all this about "causeway"? We never heard any talk of this before.'

'True ...'

'Before this, it was always the Barriers, the Barriers. Now, it is the Causeway . . . I tell you, Domenico, that man looked like a politician. Orlando. Salandra. Churchill. Clemenceau. All these crappy politicians that lead men into war. Their noses grow every time they open their mouths.'

Domenico grinned. He knew Primavera well, the sudden rages the man was capable of, how quickly, too, he would settle down, forgetting the reason for his outburst.

'But there's some truth in what the man was saying ...'

'Uh ...?'

'We have no choice but to do this work. We might as well get on with it. And if it helps the people on these islands, so much the better.'

Primavera's feet halted, stopping on the edge of a great brown pool of water as he turned to face the short, round man by his side.

'You know the trouble with you, Chiocchetti? You're a bit of a causeway yourself. Always trying to build bridges to other people. Always trying to reach out.'

༃

Domenico wasn't the only one against whom that accusation could be made.

The other man who fitted that description was walking

through the camp a few nights later, trying to work out how to lessen the divide between the Italians and the others on the camp. He knew many of the Balfour Beatty workers hated the Italians, seeing them as the friends and brothers of those who were killing their own relatives. Buckland knew they wanted him to be ruthless with the Italians, especially those who had been involved in the strike. Some of his own soldiers shared that view, whispering that he was too soft on the prisoners.

Major Buckland loved Italy. He had wanted to be married there and, instead, had honeymooned there with his new bride. He had seen Rome. The Colosseum. The Vatican. Piazza di Spagna. Fontana di Trevi. Italy's history had invigorated and revived him. He had felt the same way when he had gone there as part of the 1st Battalion of the Royal Welch Fusiliers in 1917 to support the Italian forces in their fight against the Austro-Hungarian Empire that threatened to invade after their losses at the battle of Caporetto. He recalled all the impressions that Italy had left on him. There was the warmth of its colours: the red-tiled roofs, the pink and green buildings, the awesome blue shades of its sky. He could even recall how one of the local policemen, the carabinieri, produced an orange from under the contours of his cloak, and how an old woman had danced beside the troop as they marched: 'Thank you . . . Thank you . . . Thank you for being here, *Inglesi*. Thank you . . .'

There was the difference, too, between this field of conflict and the one where he had fought before. The flat, dull shades of the Western Front. The bloody tedium of all the battles there. That sense of even the clouds never shifting, remaining as motionless at the enemy lining up in front of them, never moving from the trenches. It lightened his heart to be somewhere else, part of an army capable of moving forward instead of being fixed in the one place.

The Italian prisoners reminded him of all that, being part of a new and colourful kaleidoscope rather than being trapped within the cold and damp of the Western Front. There were times when he would speak to them in Italian, knowing that he was sometimes barely coherent in that language, but trying his best to be understood. It was a contingent of navy men he spoke to first, part of a submarine crew. They seemed to be the most isolated of all the men, as if they felt as much imprisoned by being on the land as they did being in a prisoner-of-war camp. There was also the fact that he too had been a sailor, running away from his home in Bangor with its fine castle and cathedral to work as a ship's steward on the White Star Line when he was very young.

'I need you to do me a favour,' he asked the Italian submarine captain that afternoon. 'I want someone to teach me the Italian word for the stars.'

The man had thick, brown, wavy hair and a big, round face which seemed to grow even larger when he heard the question he had been asked. 'Stars? *Non capisco.*'

'Stars. *Stelle. Seren* in Welsh. It's just that they seem so clear and bright in this part of the world. Not the way we see them in the cities. Clouded by the light.'

'Ah . . .'

'They're wonderful. There's an American writer, Emerson, who wrote, "If the stars should appear but one night every thousand years how men would marvel and stare."' He tried his best to translate but stopped when he saw the look on the captain's face. 'I want you to teach me the words for them tonight.'

'Sorry?'

'The Milky Way . . . The Plough . . . Pole Star . . .'

Again, there was a puzzled expression.

'Don't worry. I'll call for you. Take you out of the hut tonight.' He turned to the soldier who was standing by his side. 'MacAulay will arrange it tonight. Won't you?'

'Yes, sir,' the soldier said.

'Good . . .'

It was for that reason Buckland was out walking round the

camp, looking at the huts that surrounded him later that night. He knew there were men who rarely slept within them. The problem wasn't just the lack of personal space, the straw-filled mattresses, or the fact that the only heat came from the pot-bellied stoves in the middle of the room. Some of the men woke night after night when terror ripped and tore apart their dreams, or when nightmares shook their companions who dozed in the beds far too close by in the cramped quarters. Their fears took on different forms in the shadows of the room. At one moment, it might be a recollection of the war they fought. A soldier who had brandished his rifle in their direction. A broken, shattered body by their side. The next it could be the thought of their wife's infidelity. A girlfriend or sister laughing in the bed of a German soldier she had met. Their knuckles would tense as such thoughts flashed through their mind, a small betrayal of their anxieties; a groan revealing their despair.

Buckland's contemplation came to an end when MacAulay arrived at his side with the prisoners. He heard their footsteps echoing among the other noises in the camp, even the surge of the sea nearby as it washed against the length of the barrier that now stretched between Lamb Holm and the Orkney mainland.

'Ah, you're here,' he said. His attention turned to the crisp, bright stars in the night sky. 'Very good . . .' Looking at the submarine captain, he pointed into the darkness. 'We call that the Milky Way. *Llwybr Llaethog* in my other language, Welsh. What do you call it?'

'*Non capisco . . .*'

'We call that the Milky Way. What do you call it?'

'*Ah . . .*' It was clear the Italian understood. '*La Via Lattea . . .*'

He pointed in the direction of the Plough. 'What do you call that?'

'*Grande Carro . . .* Or . . .' He paused for a moment, his fingers circling as he searched for a phrase. '*Orsa Maggiore . . .*'

'The Great Bear. Yes. Yes. *Capisco. Capisco . . .*' It was then

Buckland's attention was caught by a streak of white light moving across the sky before it died away into darkness. 'A shooting star. What do you call a shooting star?'

'A shooting star?'

'Yes . . .' He did a quick movement with his open hand before clenching it into a fist. 'A shooting star.'

The submarine captain nodded. 'We call it *lacrime di San Lorenzo.*'

'*Lacrime di San Lorenzo.* The tears of St Lawrence?'

'*Si. Si. Uno dei nostri martiri.*'

'One of your martyrs. Yes. Yes. That's lovely . . .'

His speech stilled to a halt as some other phenomenon caught his attention in the darkness. 'It's a busy sky . . . I don't think I've ever seen one with quite as much going on,' he muttered, trying to work out what was happening in a distant edge of the heavens. There was a green light, growing and shimmering. For a moment, he believed it might be something to do with the war, a German plane taking off from Norway to launch a raid on Scapa Flow, but he swiftly dashed the thought from his head. The bright luminous glow had not been created or fashioned by man, the way it began to leap and dance beyond such capabilities. One moment it seemed to resemble a lady's fan; the next a feather brandished in the stillness. He turned to MacAulay by his side for an answer. 'Do you know what that is, soldier?'

'I don't know the English for it is, sir. In Gaelic, we call it the *fir chlis.* The dancing men.'

'That doesn't mean anything to me. Not even in Welsh.' He continued to gaze upwards, watching as the light shifted and swirled, expanding over the sky until it seemed to be attempting to cross the darkness in much the same way as the Barriers now did, a bridge of stone that stretched across the various Sounds, all the way to South Ronaldsay. There seemed now to be a hint of purple in its glow. Finally, he smiled. 'I know what it is.' His blue eyes glowed with a sudden certainty. 'Aurora Borealis.'

'Aurora Borealis?'

'Yes . . . *Goleuni'r Gogledd*. The Northern Lights.' He stood there shaking his head, watching the wave of colour and how it billowed and swayed above the ocean. Coming out of the north, it seemed like a fire enfolding itself, changing shape and pattern, fanning like a flame. Finally, he shook himself. 'I tell you what, MacAulay. Get the prisoners out and give them the chance to watch this.'

'All of them, sir?'

'Yes. Get them all out to watch this. It is something they'll remember for the rest of their lives.'

'Yes, sir. I'll do that.'

It wasn't long before they were all gathered outside the huts, looking up into infinity. Some shivered with cold as they bustled together in the darkness, unused to being outside at this time of night. Flapping arms and stamping feet, they could not wait to go back indoors again.

'*Freddo . . . Freddo . . .*' one complained. 'Cold . . . cold.'

'*Madre di misericordia . . .*'

' . . . Is this the end for Rico?'

Some of them were shivering with wonder. Among them was Domenico. His face caught some of the sky's brightness as he took in all that was happening. It was as if the seasons were changing above his head. One moment there was the bright, fresh green of spring. The next there was the gold of summer. There might even have been a rustic tint, reflecting both their uniforms and autumn. It was more arresting even than the shade of rose that sometimes tinged the crests of the Dolomites, the warm violet colour that shaded its valleys. For all the great differences between the two places, the recollection reminded him a little of home.

There was more than that. Despite the talking that was going on all around, he could hear the sound of the sea more clearly than he had ever heard it before. It was as if daylight muffled it, softening the persistent echo of the waves. He remembered words the priest back in Moena had read out from the pulpit one Sunday. At the time, he hadn't really recognised their meaning. The mountains around their homes limited the wide stretch of the heavens and set up a high barrier against the sight and sound of a distant sea. He saw them now, however, understood the weight and importance of each phrase and verse:

Domine deus meus magnificatus es; vehementer confessionem et decorum induisti. Amictus lumine sicut vestimento; extendens caelum sicut pellem; qui tegis aquis superiora eius. Qui ponis nubem ascensum tuum; qui ambulas super pennas ventorum . . .

O Lord my God, you are very great; you are clothed with splendour and majesty. He wraps himself in light as with a garment; he stretches out the heavens like a tent and lays the beams of his upper chambers on their waters. He makes the clouds his chariot. You walk on the feathers of the winds.

It was while these words were going round his head that he thought about the possibility of a church. Buckland had offered one of the Nissen huts for use as both a school and church. For all the kindness of the offer, he didn't want that – the two worlds alongside each other. He knew they were both necessary, but they should be kept apart. The sacred and the secular. The altar and the teacher's desk. The church needed its own space, its own intimacy to allow the voice of God to truly speak, not to jostle alongside the words of others.

'*Chiedo permesso di parlare* . . . Permission to speak, sir . . .'

He was in front of Buckland before he knew it, stammering out his request that the church should have its own separate building. He rushed out his reasons for his view: that the church should be a special place, set apart from others. Yet the more he spoke, the more his ability to speak deserted him. The intensity of the man's blue eyes served only to intimidate him. He wished that the commander could speak his own language, Ladin, or even had proper Italian, and not the garbled tongue he possessed. He could persuade him then.

'There is no reason why not.'

He turned on his heels when he heard the Englishman say this word. 'No . . .' The palms of his hands were clammy, his fingers hot and sweaty. Even gravity felt as though it were slipping away from him.

'*Tutro il a detra* . . . Okay. All right . . .' he repeated.

Buckland stared in his direction when he walked away, wondering why the man's face was clouded with disappointment, why there was a heaviness in the prisoner's step. He had said it would be fine to have the chapel in a separate Nissen hut, that there was no reason why a church could not be built. That was what he had wanted, wasn't it?

If so, why didn't he look pleased?*

࿇

Even the birds seemed to mock the prisoners that summer.

Gulls would gather nearby when they worked on the causeway, jabbing their beaks in the direction of the men, as if they insulting them with jibes. Fulmars would nest on the grassy slopes near Lamb Holm, swirling over the men from time to time. When anyone went near the nests, they would puff up their necks, gathering oil to spit at the intruders. Occasionally, too, there would be the 'hoodie crows', their dark eyes gleaming as they watched the men at their labours, greeting every movement they made with a raucous caw. The Italian soldiers felt once again as if they were at the tail end of things. The end of the causeway. The end of the war. The end of the world. The end of the Fascist regime and its mad dreams.

---

* This part of the story is an invention. It should be noted that there is a little confusion between various testimonies in the Orkney papers of the time. As these were recorded 14 years after the end of the Second World War, it is hardly surprising.

Many of them had seen all that coming for years. There were the soldiers who had witnessed the reality of the Italian Empire in Abyssinia and known then the grand scale of Mussolini's delusions. For others, the moment of realisation had come when they heard of Il Puzzone stepping onto his balcony of the Piazza Venezia in Rome one last time in December 1941 and declaring war on the United States of America. A frail husk of the man he once was, he pounded the edge of the balustrade and, attacking Roosevelt, declared: 'One man, one man only, a real tyrannical democrat, through a series of infinite provocations, betraying with a supreme fraud the population of his country, wanted the war and had prepared for it day by day with diabolical obstinacy.'

The words trailed and echoed across the dwindling crowd, convincing no one who stood there. From the faltering, hesitant way he spoke, it was doubtful that he even deceived himself. Among those who were familiar with their new enemy, both its industrial might and the power of its cinema, there would have been a shrug, the framing of a familiar question. 'Mother of Mercy, is this the end for Il Duce?'

Over the next few months, it became apparent that it might be. By the end of March, the Italian soldiers might have glimpsed American ships arriving in Scapa Flow, preparing to join the war in Europe. Among the first to arrive was an aircraft carrier, the USS *Wasp* together with the heavy cruiser, the USS *Wichita*. Both ships were guided into port by HMS *Edinburgh*, one of many Royal Navy vessels now sheltering in Orkney, used to protect the Arctic convoys or ships making their way to Iceland and America's eastern seaboard. They were safe now that a barrier was in place, preventing any German ships or U-boats slipping in and out of the harbour.

Above the camp the men could see and hear warplanes using Orkney's many airports. Like a noisier, larger version of the greylag geese they often saw flying over the island, the planes took off at all times of day and night, making their presence known to those who tried to work or sleep below. Their intention was to harass Hitler's ships, protect merchant vessels, and attack German-occupied Norway.

Among them was the Gloster Gladiator, one of the last biplanes ever flown by the Royal Air Force and Royal Navy. It was the first British plane to touch down on an American aircraft carrier during the conflict. If any of the Italians had caught sight of it, they would have recognised it as a sign of the nightmare that might be about to descend on their families at home.

They cursed the Fascists and all that their pomp and vanity had brought to pass, knowing that they could expect no kindness or consideration from their rulers. They remembered what Il Duce had declared to the Chamber of Deputies many years before: 'Fortunately the Italian people are not habituated to eating several times a day.'

The men could sense that their families were already suffering greatly at home, judging by the small clues left behind in their letters they received after they had been censored by the authorities. Bread was being rationed. Petrol, soap and coffee were almost unobtainable.

One of the soldiers tried to comfort his fellow countrymen by joking that these shortages had been happening for years. 'The bigger and bigger the Empire got, the less and less coffee we got for our cups. There must be some connection . . .'

'Perhaps Il Duce is gulping it all,' another made a quick rejoinder.

There was a rueful laugh. They knew only too well how the regime would seek to embolden their people, not with food but with empty, meaningless slogans. They dimly repeated them in their own heads sometimes, like a futile prayer to a god who had lost – or never possessed – any meaning in their lives.

'War is to the male what childbearing is to the female.'

'Let us have a dagger between our teeth, a bomb in our hands, and an infinite scorn in our hearts.'

'*Fino alla vittoria.* Until the victory.'

Until that particular dream was over, however, they knew that they were still regarded as the enemy by those who guarded them. Once or twice, they gave them reason to feel that way. On a particularly miserable Orkney morning, the men of one Nissen hut decided they had spent enough time quarrying stone and mixing concrete under the lash of rain and storm, refusing to place even a well-shod foot out of doors. Despite all appeals, they failed to shift their toes from their quarters for the remainder of the day either, remaining tight within their blankets instead. It was 11 p.m. before they were stirred from them, disturbed by the arrival of the guards an hour after lights out. As they stood beside their beds, their belongings were searched thoroughly before they were allowed to return to the warmth of their mattresses. An hour later, the pantomime began again. The prisoners were turfed out of their beds, their belongings scrambled through once again. It was a routine that continued throughout the night, each hour bringing this false reveille, the clatter of yet more soldiers' boots to their sleeping quarters. One man was so annoyed at being disturbed that he tried to bite a guard's thumb as he turned down the blankets.

'*Vattene via! Via al diavolo!... Ma che? Siamo tutti somari?* Do you think I'm a donkey?'

And then there was the single attempt at escaping from Camp 60. A group of men, in their wisdom, decided to ignore Orkney's position on the map, the way the storms and violence of the seas that surrounded the islands made it difficult even to contemplate the prospect of escaping from its borders. Finding a wrecked dinghy on the east end of Lamb Holm, they set about repairing it, determined that it might provide a means to make the journey home. No one could describe it as seaworthy, and yet they stocked up on food, scrimping on rations. Soon after, allegedly, one of the prisoners produced his masterstroke. Pretending to want to study geography, he managed to obtain an atlas from a shop in Kirkwall.

It was with the aid of this that he planned to row to Norway – or, perhaps, Italy. Fortunately for their survival, they did not end up like Pinocchio and Geppetto in the belly of some hungry shark. Their frequent outings to the east of the island were noted by the guards. The boat was soon discovered; the aspiring mariners stranded on land once again.

Despite small rebellions like these, the prison camp regime was not particularly repressive. As Deputy Camp Commander James Booth pointed out in the book *Churchill's Prisoners*, they were 'subject to the same rules and regulations as any British army camp. Reveille was at 6 a.m. in the summer, but at daylight in the winter months; lights-out at 10 p.m. Occasionally, there was an extra roll-call after the men returned from work, just to keep them up to scratch. There was also the occasional search, but these were infrequent. Main items of confiscation were British money or any type of weapon that might have been manufactured by the prisoners.'

There was risk, though, to their work, a cost borne largely by the men employed by Balfour Beatty. One Italian had died of pneumonia while he was there – a victim, no doubt, of the constant dampness of the place. Another man, Giovanni Scarponi, had been killed in a freak accident. One of the skilled workers, he was the driver of a diesel locomotive. He had been starting up its engine when it backfired, the starting handle striking him on the head and fracturing his skull. A dash to Balfour Hospital in Kirkwall had not saved him. Like the man who died from pneumonia, he was buried in Orquil Cemetery with full military honours. Following the war, their bodies were exhumed and returned to Italy.

Most of the men tried to divert themselves from all thought of their imprisonment by keeping themselves active. Some chose sport to do this. Others played music on the variety of instruments – including accordions, zithers, and Domenico's mandolin – found in the camp. Like others, Domenico sometimes escaped from the camp's realities by making mischief and playing pranks on the guards. There was one occasion when, together with others, he captured one of the gulls that gathered around them continually. Looking for spare bits of food, he and his friends trapped it with some bread impaled on a fish hook. Taking it into the hut where he worked, they brought two cans of paint. One was green; the other red. Slowly, he daubed one shade on each wing. Another man was laughing as he held the seagull's neck.

'We'll have to wait a moment till it dries,' he said.

It didn't take long. The other man giggled as he went round the back of the hut, the bird trapped below his arm. Domenico stepped in the direction of the guard.

'Italian airplane . . .'

'*De?*' The guard shot him a questioning look, imagining a fighter plane or bomber weaving its way through cloud and barrage balloon towards Scapa Flow. 'Where? What do you mean?'

His finger pointed in the direction of the gull, flying above the hut. 'There!'

The flap of multicoloured wings took the guard by surprise. 'What?' he shouted, his finger tightening on his trigger as he saw it rise. It was a moment or two before he realised what it was – that yellow beak with the bloodstain at its tip, the shades of the Italian flag disguising the greyness of its wings. The guard laughed as the rifle was lowered.

'You had me fooled for a moment there . . .' he grinned.

However, Buckland wasn't pleased. For once, his blue eyes grew steely with anger. With a few brief words, he ordered Domenico to be sent to the punishment block outside the perimeter. He was put on a diet of bread and water for three days.

Mostly, Domenico learned to avoid despair through work. He spent many of his hours painting in the hut. It was his role to create posters and news-sheets like *Sole D'Italia*, helping to decorate its pages with little sketches such as one of Cupid sitting on a silent artillery gun pointing an arrow in the direction of the foe. There is even a cartoon sketch of Pinocchio's cricket found among the papers in the camp. He illustrated, too, the scenery for the camp's entertainment, especially shows organised by men from the north of Italy. (The southern prisoners tended to like material from their own part of the country, finding this easier to comprehend.) They put on operettas, concerts, marionette and theatrical performances for the prisoners and the soldiers in the camp. One was for a production of the operetta, *The Baker Of Venice*, in which colourful gondolas moved slowly across the stage. A number of important guests, including the landowner, P.N. Sutherland Graeme, Lord Lieutenant of Orkney, and his family came to see this production. They brought with them a bouquet of flowers from behind their walled garden for use in every scene.*

With this bright array of colours around him, Domenico tried to fool himself that he was back in Moena once again. The Ladin people had a wonderful tradition of masques and carnivals. He had often seen in his youth the *Lachees*, handsome young men who led the parades, wearing hats decorated with silver coins, mirrors, feathers and the ribbons they had been given by the young women of the village. Holding masks and long staffs in their hands, they were followed by the *Marascon* who wore ringing cowbells around their chests and waists. Wearing the Ladin national costume with buckled shoes, black leather trousers, white socks and green jacket, they leapt around, adding their own noise and merriment to the proceedings. And then, wearing a longer-nosed mask than any of the others, was the *Buffon*. He waved rattle-sticks in one hand while in the other, he carried a spyglass which he pointed in the direction of all the unmarried girls around. A moment or two later and he leapt to their sides, whispering compliments or

---

* Their compatriots in Camp 34 on Burray put on an even more elaborate production with scenery that was designed to represent a three-storey palazzo. It had windows at the top which the singers popped their heads through, giving the impression of height.

insults into their ears. Wherever he went, he created laughter and amusement in his wake.

Each of these figures added their own hues to life in the Fassa valley in winter and summertime. Domenico recalled some of their colours each time he lifted his brush, using them as part of the kaleidoscope of shades he employed to paint the posters and scenery. But there was more nowadays even than that. Slowly, he seemed to be beginning to draw some inspiration from the island around him, the small graces and wonders he had failed to notice when he first arrived because of the torrential rain, the perpetual wind. There was the green of the Orkney landscape. The sparkling blue of the sea surrounding him. The wide stretch of the horizon with the mountains of Scotland like purple stitches at their edge. They all seemed to form layers on top of one another, the ocean mirroring them all. He began to enjoy the sense of space they gave him, a different kind of beauty from all he had witnessed at home.

There were times when he noticed how a gleam of sunshine hurried across the land. Occasionally cloud might block it, darkening the light, but a second later, it was back on display again – fading, appearing, disappearing, unpredictable in the way it moved across a green field or the coastline. He rejoiced sometimes in its lack of constancy, the way it kept shifting and changing as it danced across the earth. It was among the wonders he kept watching on the island, giving him a fresh view of the world.

He knew he was fortunate in many ways. As one of the 30 or so members of staff, he stayed in a smaller hut than most of the men, one with 15 beds instead of 50. He didn't have to put on oilskins, boots and gloves to head out to work in all weathers. His hands didn't bleed or become cracked as they manhandled concrete. Instead, he spent much of his day copying out documents, making sure that relevant information was passed on. He would watch the others work on the road, assisting the lorry drivers with their loads, ensuring the dumping took place in the right area. They waved their arms like windmills as the drivers manoeuvred, making sure they reversed safely. There were others, too, fashioning concrete blocks, checking that both electricity and lorry engines were operating well. He painted this sometimes – a picture, perhaps, of a semaphore signaller standing nearby when a cement block was ready to be hoisted into position. They did all this under the observant eye of men like C. Gordon Nicol, the man who was in charge of the entire operation, anxious that all was in order.

And as the summer progressed, it became possible for more and more of the people of Burray and South Ronaldsay to begin to dream of taking tentative steps across the thin barrier of rock, making their way to the Mainland. Some of them may have complained a little about this, the shopkeepers of St Margaret's Hope, perhaps. They saw the possibility of mobile vans making their way across the Barriers, bringing goods that they themselves sold, and at cheaper prices. Maybe, too, the housewives of South Ronaldsay would begin to pay visits to the distant metropolis of Kirkwall. Before this, much of their world had lain within the limits of their own small islands. Now, all of Orkney lay before them, the sweet and heady possibilities of St Mary's, Kirkwall and – even – Stromness. When it was first possible to walk across in August 1943, they seemed barely able to trust the solidity of the ground below them. It was as if a miracle had been performed, transforming liquid into solid stone, salt into concrete. One of the relatives of Annie Robson who had been lost years before might have stopped as he or she crossed Kirk Sound, saying a hushed prayer into the wind, looking down into the depths.

There were delights, too, in the way that thin thread of rock began to bring people together. Some lorry drivers broke regulations and took Italian prisoners to and from Kirkwall long before the end of the war was declared. Integration was slower for the POWs on Lamb Holm, that uninhabited isle, than it was for the prisoners who lived on Burray and who had been part of the local community for a long time, their camp not far from the road running through the centre of the island. Day after day, they had seen the people of the community working in their fields or on their homes and had volunteered to help. One Italian prisoner had lifted up a scythe and waded into the centre of a field full of hay. The local men had watched with astonishment as he cut a spiral through the grass, starting in the middle and working his way slowly out.

'That's not the Orkney way . . .' he had been told gently but firmly. 'Not the Orkney way at all.'

On another occasion, a little girl walking with her mother had been presented with a silver ring shaped out of a sixpence. From the expression on his face, it was clear the prisoner was delighted to see a child once again, one that, perhaps, reminded him of his own growing up in Italy without him. '*Bambina*. Beautiful *bambina*,' he kept saying.

Yet through all that time, there were still uncertainties, especially when they overheard whispers about how the war was going, watching warships bristling with guns setting out for places that did not seem in these times all that far from home – Gibraltar, Malta, the Mediterranean, North Africa. The end of the war did not seem that far away either. By the middle of the Orkney summer, all their uncertainties started to fade. News began to reach the prisoners that the Allied forces had invaded Sicily, the name of the city of Messina being mentioned again and again. (One of the guards had said that it was the first time the Yanks had seen real fighting – not the fake kind in these daft films they watched.) Later, too, the city of Rome was bombed, enemy aircraft swirling like unstoppable, indestructible birds over the nation's capital. Their colours were different from the ones that shaded Domenico's seagull. Rings of red, white and blue and giant stars decorated their wing-tips, signifying they were part of the Royal Air Force or the US Air Force. Their shadows fell across places like the Piazza Venezia, where Mussolini's followers had gathered many years before when the movement was at its zenith. Now, those whom Frederico Felicetti had once derided as '*canalins*' scurried away for shelter, anxious not to lose their lives because of the follies of their leader. With each day that passed, even the few that remained loyal had lost their trust in the man. On the 25 July 1943, his reign came to an end. The Grand Council of Fascism met with Mussolini to tell him that his days in power were over. King Victor Emmanuel III even sent out one of his carabinieri to arrest him as he left the Royal Palace, imprisoning him at Campo Imperatore, an Apennine ski resort not far from Rome.

'You are the most hated man in the country,' the king was reputed to have told him. 'Your soldiers in the Alpini brigade are said to be singing a song about you. Its chorus goes "Down with Mussolini, who murdered the Alpini."'

Mussolini did not answer, remembering, perhaps the enthusiastic songs that had echoed across the Palazzo Venezia when the conflict had just begun. He recalled the words '*Centurie, Coorti, Legioni, In piedi che l'ora suonò! . . .*' booming wherever he went. There was no echo of that remaining. Instead, the crowds only displayed enthusiasm when an announcement hummed and crackled on the radio.

> His Majesty the King-Emperor has accepted the resignation, from the office of Head of Government and Chief Secretary of State, of His Excellency Cavaliere Benito Mussolini . . .

In the streets of Rome, there was cheering and dancing. Fascist symbols were hacked from walls. Enormous portraits of Mussolini were thrown out of the windows of *Il Messaggero*, the Party newspaper. For the first time in years, the prisoners were free to express what they really felt. Grinning in the direction of their guards, they would stick up their thumbs and declare: 'Churchill – very good man. Mussolini – very bad man.'

Yet for all that his regime was now over, there was still no end to uncertainty among the men. The war still appeared to be going on under Badoglio, Mussolini's successor, for all that his fellow countrymen were reluctant to continue to engage in it. Rumours circled among the prisoners with all the constancy of the seagulls overhead, crying loud in alarm from time to time. They seemed to feast on any small titbit of information gleaned from a newspaper article or dropped from the lips of anyone who was in the vicinity. There were some things they were certain about. Many of the people at home were hungry. Fire and shells rained down on many of the towns and cities they had left. Suffering haunted both farm and street, particularly in the nation's south. The smell of Il Puzzone and his Blackshirts might have faded from the scene, but enough of his foulness still remained, permeating the entire country.

It left its mark, too, on the men in the camp. The tedium of waiting for the coming of peace had its own terrors. There were nights when storms rattled over the roofs of their huts like landslides in the Dolomites, altering the shape of the landscape. Some shouted out, yelling out the names of their loved one. Others tensed their fists when they saw a native of the opposite end of Italy. They were aware that their nation was more divided than ever. To the north, they knew that there were still German troops. In the south, the British and Americans held sway. In the camps people withdrew into groups formed around a shared home-town or region. Men like Domenico, who were peaceful by nature, walked more and more tentatively, as if moving across a thin, precarious ledge somewhere near his home, terrified that if his foot stepped out too boldly, he would topple and fall into the abyss. By a single, clumsily expressed word, a stone might be dislodged, echoing in the gorge below, causing injury to others.

However, their greatest fears surrounded those matters about which they were most doubtful: the politics of their native land. What would the Blackshirts do now that power had been taken from their leader? Would war continue? Would the Germans turn their guns on those they had previously marched beside? They skimmed the pages of *Il Corriere Del Prigioniero*, the newspaper they received regularly from London, and listened, too, to the radio in the Balfour Beatty camp which they were allowed to hear throughout the war.

There was little doubt that more and more German troops were moving south through the Brenner Pass, unable to rely on the Italians any more. Some of the prisoners recalled the small resentments they had always endured when they were together in the African desert: their awareness that their partners in the Pact of Steel always had better equipment than them, even more food to fill their stomachs. They had felt uneasy even then, irritated by those who were meant to be on their side. They distrusted them more, though, as opponents, certain they would be brutal, bloody and callous, especially against Italians, a race whom they had never really respected, more often despised. In their darkest nightmares, those nights when the endless drumming of the rain echoed on roofs and windows, they feared what might happen when the inevitable happened – that Italians, sick of the war and all its madness, would lay down their guns or turn them against the forces to which they had acted as unwilling hosts for too long.

Domenico found his own way of keeping doubts and demons at bay. It was around that time he began to work on the statue of St George slaying the dragon near the entrance to the camp. It was something that Buckland immediately granted him permission to do. In fact, Buckland was the one who suggested the figure, an uncontroversial choice for the Calvinist Scots who would see it everyday. 'It's the national symbol of the English,' he said, 'No doubt those who serve here will enjoy seeing it. A souvenir of home. God knows that some of them moan enough about being this far north. It might help to keep them quiet.' He gave a dry chuckle. 'Mind you, I don't know if I should approve of it. I was brought up in the north of Wales. Our emblem is the dragon. The very thing that St George kills.'

Domenico didn't speak in response. He knew the saint also belonged to the cities of Milan and Genoa. As a warrior-hero, put to death by Diocletian in AD 303, he was connected with the military too. For a thousand reasons, he was the one Domenico had chosen to sculpt. According to his fellow prisoner Bruno Volpi, it was also meant to be 'a concrete representation of the desire to eliminate all wars, all wars that cause pain and injustice to so many people. It is the symbol of a will to "kill" all misunderstandings between people of different cultures.'

Domenico thought about it for a while, perhaps remembering his life in the Dolomites when he drew his initial sketches, recalling the misunderstandings and misapprehensions that had come to divide the people there. And then there was the larger, greater conflict that men like Mussolini had caused as they marched their people into battle on their Field of Miracles. He could hear the moans and murmurs of the men when bad news somehow managed to reach them even in this isolated place or they recalled moments when their friends were lost.

It wasn't long before he went to work on the sculpture, fashioning its frame from barbed wire, shaping a horse, a man in armour and helmet, till slowly, surely, the form of a knight and his steed was created. In the beginning, an iron framework held it aloft, preventing the rider from toppling downwards, the wire from scraping and cutting his face as it fell. A spear was tucked below St George's arm, one that plunged its own barbed tip into the beast that was below hooves, trampling downwards as the dragon's head reared up, trying to ward off its attacker. Buttapasta came to assist him, covering the framework with the cement left over from that day's work, which was so plentiful in the camp, giving it greater and greater girth. Soon it took on the shape of a large cemented man.

Cement was a resource they used for everything. They cast a table and desk in concrete, and built an outdoor bowling alley with concrete skittles. Even the legs of the billiard table where some of the men played during their leisure hours depended on vast quantities of cement to stay upright, the concrete balls and stick clicking as they spun in the direction of the small fragment of fishing net at the corners and sides. There would be a cheer as a black was potted, echoing across the room.

They built a plinth for St George too, one that was in position for 7 August 1943, some time before Italian capitulation was announced. The names of the prisoners held at Camp 60 were noted on a sheet contained within it. They plugged this in a bottle, together with some Italian notes and coins. And then they gathered round it, having their photograph taken. No doubt some of them considered the statue odd, placed there on the edge of the camp. No church walls sheltered it. It was not in a city piazza where pigeons might gather and land. Instead, it gazed out over the sea, the treeless fields of Orkney. Nevertheless, its presence among them reminded some a little of the homes they had left. In a land which seemed bereft of statues or man-made art, its very presence made a statement about how different the nation they had left was from its immediate surroundings. They applauded and cheered when it was unveiled, set flowers around it, knowing that in some ways, Domenico and Buttapasta had created a work of art that was in itself a statement of man's ability to escape the boundaries laid down by walls and barbed wire, showing, in Bruno Volpi's words, that when people were 'down in spirit, physically and morally deprived of many things, one could still find within oneself something that could be set free'.

But Domenico needed more than his art, the congratulations of both guards and fellow prisoners when the sculpture was finished and put in place. The need for something greater than all of these things was within him, a need rooted in the small church in Moena where he had spent the Sundays of his childhood and the other churches and cathedrals he had witnessed in his youth. He wished to see the murals once again, to hear, too, the words of a priest from his altar, granting a focus for Christ's flock.

News began to reach him that this might happen, his wishes might be granted. There were stories of the coming of a priest to the island to look after the welfare of the prisoners. He didn't dare believe the stories at first, dismissing them from his thoughts. But hope kept creeping into his head, becoming more and more persistent. He looked forward to the day the Church might be restored to his life, a priest before the altar, consecrating bread and wine with the words:

Hoc est enim Corpus Meum. Hic est enim Calix Sanguinis mei, novi et aeterni testamenti: mysterium fidei: qui pro vobis et pro multis effundetur in remissionem peccatorum.

They were words that might appease his restlessness of spirit, restoring and healing him, providing a sense that God's peace might be coming, that he might soon go home.

7

CAUSEWAYS

CHAPEL LIGHTS

They'd scrape the least, last bite of meat
out of corned beef tins,
making sure no morsel left behind
would soil the gleam within,

and then they'd hammer, cut and snip
that metal till they made
holders for these candles
in which light could be displayed

below a chain rippling with stars
they imagined could be seen
the length of their peninsula –
Milano, Roma, Torino,

from the southern edge of Sicily
to snow-crisp Dolomites,
till Mediterranean nights were canned within
each gleaming tin of light.

'At this point he went to look in the mirror, and he thought he was someone else. No longer did he see the usual reflection of a wooden marionette; instead he saw the sprightly and intelligent image of a handsome boy with brown hair, blue eyes, and an expression so happy you'd have thought it was his birthday.

'Amid all these marvels coming one right after the other, Pinocchio no longer knew whether he was awake or just dreaming with his eyes open . . .'

For all that a heavy downpour was blurring the distinction between sky and the sea surrounding them, Domenico was grinning, thinking of the slow, stumbling way one of the scholar's students had read aloud the final chapter of Carlo Collodi's classic book within one of the huts the other day. There was something in its words that chimed with the way he felt about all that had happened over the last few months. The marvels had begun with Capitulation Day a few months before. That news had come through at the beginning of September. With its arrival, it was as if the humanity of the prisoners had been restored. The 'target' discs that had decorated their uniform were removed that day: a few items of furniture added to the canteen; a radio provided. For the first time, too, the Italians were paid in real money, not discs printed with '½d' or '1d' or notes that resembled those from a Monopoly box as they had received previously.* As they walked around the camp that day, watching the football match that was going on for the first time against their compatriots in Burray, several must have jingled the coins in their pockets, feeling that through this simple transaction, their reflections in the looking glass had been given back to them once more. They were no longer prisoners of war. The same authorities watched over them, caring for their welfare while they were still unable to go home, but there was now a greater degree of freedom in their lives.

---

* Skilled workers obtained the princely sum of 1s 6d per day during the years of the conflict; the other, more numerous unskilled men received only 1s.

It was from this time that Italians played an increasingly important part in the lives of ordinary Orcadians. Four years old at the beginning of the war, Joyce Johnstone, who grew up as Joyce Harcus on Hurtiso Farm and now lives in Kirkwall, recalled how she used to see them walking around her native parish of Holm, occasionally visiting her parents' home. They used to volunteer to work in the farm. Four young men would strip off their jackets and help in the hay. Another enjoyed milking the cattle, a reminder of his life on a farm in Italy. There would be a flurry of hand signals as he 'spoke' to Joyce's father, bilingual messages passed over the hindlegs of one of the family cows.

Clearly there would be a few cultural misunderstandings in the process. As she sits in her family home below a painting of the manse and Holm Church, her childhood in the area comes vividly to life. Her eyes shine and twinkle as she remembers the time her mother gave two of the Italian workers, Franco De Sentos and Carlo Loretta sausages and eggs on a Friday. 'One looked at the other and the other looked back, no doubt remembering it was meant to be a fast day, when only the eating of fish was permitted. A few seconds later, though, and the two of them were wolfing it all down. Not a crumb was left behind on the plate.'

There was, however, a greater legacy left behind than a memory of hard work shared, energy and endeavour. On the walls of her sitting room there is evidence both of her love of Orkney and her awareness of the world outside. Alongside the picture of Holm Church is a scroll of Japanese writing. Photographs of family members like her husband, Bertie, are displayed in the room and there is evidence, too, of the other great love in her life – music. For all that she worked in the former National Bank in Kirkwall for a number of years until her marriage and career as a home-carer, music has been one of the most significant aspects of her existence. She plays the organ in the church; her daughter is a music teacher in Kirkwall Grammar School. It is a life that has been enriched by song, but one she recognises was influenced profoundly by a Sunday afternoon when she went with her Mum and Dad to see the camp orchestra play.

Her impressions of that day tumble from her. She remembers her mother looking round the cookhouse, wrinkling her nose and describing it as 'oily' from all the varieties of pasta cooked within its walls. She remembers, too, the men of the orchestra with their home-made violins, cello, drums, how exotic and unusual they were. Most of all, however, she recalls the music, so different from the kind to which she was used to listening in Orkney. Its melody and haunting words, replete with longing for the brightness and heat of the Neapolitan sun, were transcribed and placed into her hand.

> *Ma n'atu sole,*
> *cchiù bello, oje ne'*
> *'O sole mio*
> *sta 'nfronte a te!*
> *'O sole, 'o sole mio*
> *sta 'nfronte a te!*
> *sta 'nfronte a te! . . .*

She would have seen too the members of Domenico's theatre group, La Compagnia Settentrionale, perform. Among them there would have been men like Sforza, the principal comic, and Celo Santini singing '*Ideale*', a song written by Paolo Tosti and filled with longing for peace.

> *Io ti seguii come'iride di pace*
> *Lungo le vie del cielo;*
> *Io ti seguii come un'amica face*
> *De la notte nel velo . . .*

> I followed you like a rainbow of peace
> A long way across the sky;
> I followed you like a friendly face
> Of the night under a veil . . .

There was a different sort of artistry and craft in some of the objects fashioned by the men. Models of Spitfires and Hurricanes swirled above humble ashtrays. Sculptures of Christ on the cross were miraculously placed in glass bottles. Models of Milan Cathedral were constructed from matchsticks. There were beautifully engraved tea-trays made from wood or scrap aluminium and the ubiquitous cigarette lighters. Joyce remembers her father buying three heavy ones for £5 from one of the prisoners. Later, he sold a pair of them elsewhere for £7 10s.

Near the end of the war, her family also received an unusual leaving gift from the Italians. A large cat they later called 'Tubby' arrived, tucked up in the arms of one of the former prisoners a few days before their departure.

'Could you take it?' he asked.

Later, they discovered that Tubby hid a number of important secrets within her fur: she was pregnant with four kittens. She possessed the ability to stand on her hind legs begging for the occasional titbit. She used to lie on top of the radio, waiting for the family car to arrive home. It was as if she were tuning into the strange voices from the box below, hoping that the dial might be shifted, enabling her to hear the speech of her former Italian masters again.

At his home in South Ronaldsay, George Esson the local historian and undertaker told me a few similar stories about the craftwork of the prisoners. The most moving, however, involved the response of one of the men when provided with his dinner within their home one day. The young Italian had started to cry with joy at the kindness he had been shown. When George's father questioned him, he choked out the reason why he was behaving that way. 'Like my family ... People again ... I am people again.'

Like the other Italians, Domenico would have known exactly what he meant by remarks like these. He might have seen his old self as Pinocchio saw the puppet, his head barely upright, arms dangling, dressed in a rustic uniform with patches sewn onto its back, kneecaps and elbows.

'How sad I looked when I was a prisoner. And how happy I feel now that I've become a free man again.'

And then he would think back to one of these moments that restored him to all he had been before . . .

～

The cold cut through Father Gioacchino Giacobazzi as he stepped from the lorry that late September morning, having suffered an uncomfortable journey across the Barriers a few moments before. Its asphalt surface wasn't ready yet. He had noticed many of his fellow countrymen employed on it, wielding pick-axes and spades. Some of them were working, too, in the Rockworks factory with its bars of iron, mounds of cement and coal. They glanced his way when he looked in their direction, not approaching because, he decided, their spirits were low from working in such cold and alien conditions. A wave of pity for the way they were suffering swept over him. He could remember when it had all been so different, when it seemed the Italian army were as invincible as the statue of St George killing the dragon someone had built near the camp.

He had been in Gondar, Ethiopia's former royal capital when war had been declared. Alongside its palaces, mosques and even the synagogues frequented by the city's many Jews, there were also the buildings – both Italian and modern – that surrounded the main piazza. He had loved to walk there, proud both of his faith and nationality, believing he was part of a vanguard bringing civilisation to a backward people. All around him, he had heard the soldiers of the Italian army whistling a popular tune:

> *Faccetta nera*
> *Bella abissina*
> *Aspetta e spera*
> *Gia l'Italia s'avvicina . . .*

> Little black face,
> Pretty Abyssinian girl,
> Wait and hope
> And already Italy is approaching...

It didn't take long for that song, often described as the most significant evidence of the racist element in Fascism, to fade from their lips. He saw them again lying in their hospital beds in the town of Soddu, not far from its large garrison and fort. He spent a little time attending to their needs before the troops there surrendered to the South Africans. He remembered how he had reacted when that had occurred, ordering a man to take down the Italian flag. It was still in his possession, at the bottom of his bag, when the enemy were breaking through the gates. It was an instinct born during his own service in the Great War, where he had to duck and dive in the trenches. Once, part of a grenade had even sliced through his cap.

After his capture, there was the long walk to the eucalyptus-scented streets of Addis Ababa – a journey that began in August 1942 when his patients were evacuated and escorted north-east to that city. Soon, there were other journeys, to Somaliland, Egypt, and finally to Edinburgh, where on 9 September 1943, he had stood with 30 other chaplains, waiting to be told where they were to be sent. Finally, he had been informed. 'You're going to Camp 60. Orkney.'

And so it had all come to this. A journey which had begun in heat and high fever had ended up in the North Atlantic, between Scotland and Iceland. From a time of victory and celebration to one of sorrow and defeat. A place of dryness and dust to one dominated by salt-laden winds and sea. He shivered at the thought of the contrasts he had seen over the last while, turning to the driver as he did so. 'I want to speak to Major Buckland, the camp commander.'

'Of course. I'll show you the way.'

There are few forces in this world more formidable than a determined cleric and Father Gioacchino Giacobazzi was certainly among their number. His black clothes flapped as he stepped across puddles and mud towards the camp commander's office. Even when he reached there, he did not settle for long. He stretched out a hand to greet Major Buckland, his eyes squinting through his glasses as he gave the most brief and brisk of handshakes. 'I would like to see where the place of worship is,' he said.

'You're sure about that? After such a journey, it might be best to relax for a while.'

'No, no. I am grateful for your thought, but these men have been waiting a long time for the comfort of their faith. It is not my right to delay this for a moment longer than I possibly can.'

'Of course. I understand.'

They went together to the Nissen hut that served as both the church and school. The scholar was standing at his end of the building when they arrived. He dipped his head respectfully in the direction of the priest, a habit he had never quite lost despite claiming to be against all clerics. Father Gioacchino nodded in return, and also acknowledged the presence of the two men in the classroom. They had stood up when the priest entered, their eyes gleaming at his presence.

'*Buongiorno, Padre.*'

He stretched out his hand to prevent them rising, turning to the scholar instead. 'You are trying to teach these men to read and write?'

'Yes, Father.'

'Using Pinocchio?' the priest said, glancing at the book in the scholar's hand.

'Yes,' he smiled. 'They see themselves as the puppet. Dodging school all the time.'

'It is work of great value to them. Too many of our people find reading and writing a mystery. It is one of the things that brings shame to our people. Especially those in the south. Too many of them are unable to follow the written word.'

'I agree, Father. I do my best to help them.'

'I'm sure you do.' The priest's gaze took in the makeshift altar at the other end of the building. 'But this is where men both teach and pray?'

'Yes, Father.'

'I am not sure both worlds belong together. The life of the soul and that of the mind belong to very different kingdoms.'

'Some have said this before. It has been said even to the commander before.'

'Indeed.' His eyes looked critically in the direction of Major Buckland nearby. He was talking to the soldier who had accompanied them. At the same time, the British officer was doing his best to follow the other Italian conversation that was going on, far too rapidly for his understanding. Occasionally, he would look up, squinting with suspicion at the cleric in their midst. 'Who was the man who spoke about this?'

'Domenico. A man from a place called Moena. In the Alto Adige.'

'Yes. I must go and see him. He is clearly someone to whom faith is important.'

'Yes. There is little doubt about that.' He turned towards Buckland. 'I'll take you to see him. I'll ask the major if it's all right.'

'*Si. Si.* That would be good.'

A few moments later, the group was on the move again, towards the Nissen hut where Domenico and the others worked. A crow flapped before them as they did so, its harsh croak echoing as it sailed up in flight. Father Gioacchino barely acknowledged its presence. He had seen enough carrion during his time in East Africa, gathering to feast on the bodies of the dead that lay there. This one seemed mild and benign in comparison, a bird from a much kinder part of the war.

What he saw within the hut shook him, though, in a different kind of way. There were men in there hard at work, each one fashioning art and beauty with their fingers. Some even did it with their lips, the words of an anti-war song booming out.

Era nato poveretto
senza casa e senza tetto . . .

Tra la la la. Tra la la la
Tra la la la la la la la . . .

One man was painting, creating a poster for a short performance of *Cavalleria Rusticana* that was about to take place. Others were creating cigarette lighters, small models of planes, even a warship from brass and other metals, shaping these with all the skill and dexterity they possessed. They stopped working when they noticed the priest was present, looking at him with open, marvelling eyes. When they spoke, their voices were a babble of greetings, expressing welcomes that came from their lips, but echoed even more loudly in their hearts.

'*Salve, caro Padre.*'

'*Sia lodato Gesù Cristo.*'

'*Grazie a Dio, grazie a Dio . . .*'

'*Benvenuto, benvenuto, Padre.*'

He touched each one of them, grasping their outstretched fingers, noting how the marks of their trade were on them. One hand seemed to have been dipped in paint; another cut and bruised. They all seemed just small outward signs of the wounds their souls had received over the last few years. The war in the desert had inflicted that on them. The chill of these islands in the far north. So far from their homes and – worse – not amongst those who practised their faith. He had discovered they were all Protestants on this edge of the world, noting the prevalence of that particular heresy even in the plainness of the churches he had passed on his way. Cold, cold buildings, as cold as the land to which they belonged. These men with all their warmth, colour and humanity needed a great deal more than that.

When he had finished greeting them, he turned to Buckland.

'Major, these men are in desperate need of a church. Are you going to help me provide one for them?'

It took a while for Buckland to answer that question favourably.

There were a number of problems to overcome. One was the difficulty of finding space for a building on the site at Lamb Holm. Already, given the location, the buildings were tight and crammed together. The other was Major Buckland's concern that all the prisoners who were unable to read should receive schooling while they were in the camp. It was something that went back to his own early days in Bangor when he had seen young boys alongside him in the classroom who had grown up in Welsh-speaking homes struggling to master English, destined to be employed, perhaps, in the local slate works. There were, too, those years before he had run away to sea as a young man. Working as a printer's apprentice, he had watched enviously as young students made their way to the university – or 'normal' – college in the town, at that time housed in the old Penrhyn Arms Hotel on the eastern approach to Bangor. It was partly his need for similarly wide horizons that had led him to run away from home. 'School is cruel to some youngsters,' he'd declare, 'Sometimes they need to learn when they are adults. It gives them another chance.'

And then there were the many bright and educated men who needed to learn skills and exchange ideas amongst one another. School had its uses for them too, especially when they had to return home to rebuild their broken country.

Finally, however, with the assistance of C. Gordon Nicol, two Nissen huts* were connected together and their magical transformation into the Chapel began. Even in terms of their location, it must have seemed the mad and eccentric vision of a wild-eyed dreamer as they began to plan their work. On the edge

---

* The Nissen hut was the invention of Major Peter Norman Nissen in 1916. Serving with the Royal Engineers, he was the one who first thought of its semi-circular, corrugated iron design. Among its advantages were its ability to withstand bomb-blast more easily than a conventionally shaped building.

of the POW camp, it stood in a wild, exposed place that in no way resembled the part of the world they came from. The sun that so often shone above the Apennines and Dolomites rarely shone here. Both wind and sea levelled all thoughts of such majesty. The Protestant faith, in all its bareness, seemed more appropriate to the landscape in which the church would be placed.

And then there was the raw material. It was difficult to picture a simple Nissen hut with its semi-circular roof fashioned from corrugated iron ever becoming a sacred building. Its size and shape seemed to defy that possibility, too squat, low and humdrum for those who might occupy its walls to aspire to any kind of closeness to God.

Yet Domenico saw the possibility of change as clearly as the woodcutter had seen the puppet he would carve from a block of wood. With Father Gioacchino beside him, he gathered the men in the hut, those like Domenico Buttapasta, a cement worker; Palumbi, a smith; Primavera and Micheloni, the electricians; Sergeant Major Fornasier, who helped Major Buckland run the camp; Devitto... Together, they listened to the priest as he began to pray, wishing them all on their endeavour:

'*Veni, Sancte Spiritus,*
et emitte caelitus lucis tuae radium.
Veni, pater pauperum,
veni dator munerum,
veni lumen cordium ...'

'Come Holy Ghost, send down these beams which sweetly flow in silent streams from Thy bright throne above. O come, thou father of the poor, o come thou source of all our store, come fill our hearts ...'

༃

There was much to fill the hearts of the other POWs for the next few months too.

Many of them bought cheap bicycles with their wages, free-wheeling across Orkney's green farmland during the last part of that year, the beginning of the new, kicking their heels as they rolled downhill, straining every leg muscle as they pushed themselves up slopes or through a sudden onslaught of rain. New names became familiar, words like Quoyburray, Foubister, Upper Sanday, tricky for them to keep and control on their tongue. There was a whole series of new adventures for them to experience.

Ron Marwick recalled the Italian men travelling on their rickety wheels to the Strond Cinema in Holm, owned by his father J.G. Marwick. Fashioned from two large hangars that were once balloon sheds, this was a building transformed to show quite different pictures from the ones which Domenico and the others were creating within the camp.* One of the first films to be shown there was *Under Fiesta Stars*, starring Gene Autry and Barbara Erwin. Described as 'Songs, Six-Guns and Excitement', it featured 'Your Favourite Rootin' Tootin' Croonin' Cowboy And His Side-Splittin' Sidekick' singing musical numbers that took them far from the Orkney shoreline, where men could sing of how

> *We met by a stream one night in Mexico*
> *The moment stood still under fiesta stars*
> *I learned how to dream that night in Mexico*
> *My heart felt a thrill under fiesta stars...*

There were other places to which they were transported during their hours inside the Orkney equivalent of 'Cinema Paradiso': *The Road To Morocco* with Bing Crosby and Bob Hope, or perhaps *Casablanca* where Humphrey Bogart and Ingrid Bergman met again during the Second World War. Its opening credits feature a

---

* The large Nissen hut-type structure was known as a Romney shed, and only operated as a cinema for 18 months. Opening on 10 June 1943, it followed the fate of 'Cinema Paradiso' in the well-known Italian film by burning down in January 1945. Ron recalled that it had taken an age to obtain the licence for a cinema in the first place.

map of Africa, the continent which the men had left behind a few years previously. ('Waiting, waiting, waiting,' a refugee complains in the film, 'I'll never get out of here.')

They could have seen the Walt Disney version of *Pinocchio*, released for the first time in 1940. If so, they would have muttered about all the changes that the Americans had made to Collodi's original creations. 'Where did he get that silly Tyrolean hat from? . . . His nose is too short when it's not growing! . . . The Blue Fairy isn't blue. She just has blue hair! . . . The cricket's an insect. It doesn't have a top hat or cane.'

There was one film in particular that Ron Marwick recalled them watching. It arrived in its usual way from the Palace Cinema in Leith that used to book whatever reels were available. Opening their parcel that day, they discovered they had obtained a copy of the Charlie Chaplin movie, *The Great Dictator*. Father and son looked at each other momentarily before they decided they had to show the film, loading it onto their large Kalee Indomitable No. 7 projector. People expected a film to be shown. It wasn't long before they became troubled once again, noting the long line of Italian men arriving from Burray and Lamb Holm. 'I wonder how they'll take this,' his father might have said.

There was much in the film to be nervous about. There is the scene where Charlie Chaplin plays Adenoid Hynkel meeting the well-rounded figure of Benzino Napoloni for the first time. In a flurry of arms and Fascist salutes, the two have great difficulty bringing their hands into contact, missing each other's outstretched fingers each time they move towards one another. There is the moment, too, when they sit together in barber's chairs. Handles are pumped and cranked as they both try to look down on their fellow dictator while making small talk at the same time – the ultimate in oneupmanship. Behind them, their barbers stretch arms, reaching farther and farther with their scissors, anxious in the course of their struggle not to snip off either of the leaders' ears.

Way up in the projection room, Marwick senior and junior were relieved to hear the sound of laughter at some of the film's more entertaining moments. They heard a cry when the audience recognised Napoloni for who he was meant to be, stomping around, striking a match on a sculpture of Hynkel's head, and babbling in a ridiculous Italian accent. 'Il Puzzone!' they screamed. 'Il Puzzone!'

When they left the Strond Cinema, wheeling their bicycles along, the former prisoners were grinning and talking, recalling the film's finer moments like the one in which Adenoid Hynkel dances with a large, inflatable globe, caressing it and balancing it on his fingers, as if it were his partner in some kind of world ballroom dancing competition. It was, some decided, a great film with Charlie Chaplin a comic genius. Others muttered and complained that it wasn't up to much.

It is all a small reminder of something that a number of people told me while I travelled around Orkney. Even after Capitulation Day, there was some unease, dislike and even resentment towards the former prisoners in the island. For a variety of reasons, this is understandable. They were seen as having experienced a comfortable war, unlike some of the Orcadian men who may, for instance, have been imprisoned by the Japanese in the Far East. Some of their husbands and fathers, too, were in ships sunk by Italian submarines during the conflict – something which my own grandfather experienced during these years.

There was also the fact that the conflict was still going on in Italy. At the end of September 1943, the Germans had pulled off the remarkable rescue of the original Napoloni, finding the shrunken, defeated Mussolini in his own luxurious prison on the Gran Sasso. From there, they took him to Vienna, Munich, and then the Führer's headquarters in East Prussia. It was a journey that led the former Italian dictator to being placed in charge of a small German puppet state based in Salò on Lake Garda.

The man whose voice had once boomed across the Piazza

Venezia to thousands of his fellow countrymen now grumbled instead about the German soldiers who guarded him in the villa that was his home, following him, too, in their lorries and listening into his telephone calls. 'I don't want everyone to think I am a prisoner,' he complained angrily to his visitors, denying the all too apparent truth of his existence.

There were other truths which he must have tried his best to ignore or deny. When he listened to Hitler that day in his head-quarters, he could only nod his head when the German leader said that in exchange for re-establishing Fascism on Italian soil, their former partners in the Pact of Steel would need 'territorial security'. In the first stage, this consisted of the handing over of the province of Bolzano to the Third Reich. Later, perhaps, along with Trento and Belluno after a plebiscite took place in these two areas, Bolzano would become part of a new Austria. The newly annexed Dalmatia, Istria and also Trieste might have to be given up in the long term, forming what would later be known as the Adriatic Coastline. To all of this, Mussolini only listened carefully, conscious that his humiliation was not yet complete. The land he had thought to have turned into an empire was now fractured and divided. Throughout much of it, there was fighting. To the south, there were the Allied forces fighting against Germans. In its centre, the Communist partisans were doing the same. And in the far north, there was the stamp of jackboots through what was now known as the Alpine Approaches, the cobbled streets of places like the towns of the Trentino-Alto Adige, the magnificent splendour of the Dolomites. Under the Nazi rule of Gauleiter Franz Hofer, Bolzano became the place were Italian Jews were interned, a transit camp before the Jewish people were taken to the concentration camps further north and so many were slaughtered.

Few in either Lamb Holm or anywhere else in Orkney would have been aware of much of this. Some would have been conscious of a residue of bad feeling left behind after the years of war. There is evidence of this in a newspaper report that appeared in *The Orcadian* in 13 December 1984 which is headlined with the words 'Hostile Reaction Sinks POW Reunion'. Talking about the possibility of an invitation, the council convenor, Edwin Eunson, declared that he had been surprised by the amount of angry reaction to the proposal. 'I feel it is going to be a divisive issue in the county. I do not think we should proceed.' Much of this response apparently had come from local members of the British Legion, a number of whom had been imprisoned in Italy and 'not very well treated at the time'.

This anger was evident even then. A football match between the Italians and some British soldiers from the anti-aircraft batteries ended in a series of violent kicks and punches, a furore in which even the spectators became involved. One woman, Lesley McLetchie, recalled in the book *Bolsters Blocks Barriers** how her grandmother warned her not to speak to the 'dark-clothed men' working as volunteers on the farms while she travelled from Kirkwall to Burray. She supposed that this 'must have been the Italians'.

There was one particular time when this suspicion and hostility became more apparent than ever. Sandy Firth told me the story of the Battle of Shore Street, a skirmish that he had witnessed back in 1943. It was one that involved black and white, army and navy, stars and stripes (of various kinds) and finally a clash between red, blue and white, and green, white and red. As a young lad from the island of Shapinsay, he stayed in lodgings while going to school in Kirkwall. As he made his way past the town centre a little before 9 p.m. on a peaceful evening, something exploded into his life – the stained glass window of the Queens Hotel.

And then a figure landed on his back in the street. Unlike James Bond, Sandy noted, he did not get back up.

---

* This work by Alastair and Anne Cormack contains a marvellous photo-graphic record of the building of the Barriers – and much else besides.

More drama followed. Sandy had stumbled on a group of US airmen from RAF Hatston, who had spent their time drinking in the hotel between 6 p.m. and 9 p.m. They were celebrating their time away from the saloon desert of the US ship where they were based in the most wild and enthusiastic manner possible. The young lad looked round at all the various landmarks, from a urinal to a store, before performing an athletic feat even James Bond would have been proud of, scaling a seven- or eight-foot wall of sandbags that suddenly came into view. From there, he settled down with a numbers of others who had clambered up beside him to watch the melee below, trying to avoid being noticed where they lay.

There was much to see as men piled out of the hotel doorway onto the street below. He saw British soldiers wrap belts around their fists, preparing themselves for the fight. Fishermen were tugging up their sleeves. Blood and teeth were flying. The US navy and army were also showing goodwill to each other, slinging arms and boots in everyone's direction in an international free-for-all. The police put in a discreet appearance, standing on the sidelines and watching all that was going on.

It was then that the Italians turned up, walking towards the Battle of Shore Street. The others glimpsed them through their blood-battered eyes. One word slipped from their broken lips.

'EYTIES!'

The hunt was on. In an instant, those who were fighting had fixed on a single target, their former opponents in their rustic uniforms. Boots thundered in their direction. Fists clenched. Italian eyes and mouths opened in alarm. Some stumbled as they ran away, trying to rise to their feet as the drunken hordes charged towards them.

It was the US Shore Patrol, known as the Snowdrops, who put a stop to it all. Arriving on the scene kitted out in white helmet, belt and leggings, they blew whistles and swung baseball bats in the direction of these fighting, feuding men. Black or white, British, American or Italian, they toppled below their onslaught.

'Like a felled tree . . .' Sandy recalled. 'Like a forest of felled trees.'

After that, the fallen timber was lifted from the ground. A pick-up truck rolled along and the groaning bodies were thrown into the back. As soon as the sound of the engine faded from the middle of Kirkwall, Sandy and the others clambered from their position on top of the sandbags. His heart pounded, conscious that he had a story to tell his classmates the following day, aware, too, that the legend of the Battle of Shore Street was one night he would tell others about for the rest of his life.

There were other stories that could be told about the Italians during that time; a number concerning the relationships between the former prisoners and both native Orcadian women and women in the services. Some of these have been told thoroughly elsewhere. There is, for instance, the link between the blacksmith Palumbi and one particular female that is immortalised in the shape of the tiny black iron heart found at a gate-stop for the entrance to the altar in the Chapel.* Others have been whispered; allegations of illicit encounters when husbands were away from home; children who were fathered by the former prisoners. In a small community, it is important not to give too much credence to such tales. Even ripples can reverberate, affecting the living, all of whom might in some way be held to account for the actions of their forebears.

However, there are a few stories that perhaps tell us about the rather awkward qualities of the lovelorn Italians as they tried to approach some of the Orkney girls. Worshipping them from afar, they would rush up to the rather unattainable subjects of their adoration and sing them an Italian love song. At other times, they would press rings and other gifts inscribed with the words 'I Trust And Love You' into their hands, reminding them of their homeland as well as their deep affection. Sometimes the local

---

* Philip Paris fictionalises this tale in his novel *The Italian Chapel.*

women were put off by the condition and clothing of the men. In 1944, because of the shortage of wartime labour, the Italians were often employed unloading coal and other raw materials from the cargo ships that arrived in Kirkwall. Small flirtations would take place as the women in offices of employers like R. Gardens Ltd paid their new employees a few (and unofficial) shillings. '*Grazie Signorina*,' they would say, their teeth and eyes gleaming through the shroud of dust and dirt that covered them. '*Grazie*.'

There were also those who were insecure. Reminders of the women they had left at home would sometimes break into their memories, arriving there through some error or failure to control their thoughts. They imagined their young wife or fiancée walking, for instance, through a public park with an unknown man by their side. They alternated between attempting to deny these thoughts and accepting them. Wasn't it understandable that the young women whom they loved would go out and find other partners for themselves? After all, when their lives had come to a halt after they had been captured in the desert, the lives of others had gone on. And so they justified their own infidelities, even a moment of adultery or two.

Some suffered from being tongue-tied. One of the most re-markable Orcadians of the twentieth century, the self-taught folklorist and historian Ernest Marwick, witnessed one of them, a Romeo deprived of the use of his lips and tongue. In his own words, he described how it occurred.

'In 1944, when I was managing Stevenson's, one of the Italian prisoners from the Lamb Holm Camp used to come into the shop a good deal. He never said much, seldom bought much, and stood well back, often staying quite a while in the shop. One day he came in hurriedly and handed a letter to the girl who was helping me at the counter. The following is an exact copy.

Dear Miss

I am obliged to write you for telling you my feeling towards you.

Since first time I saw you; I feel something in myself that is very difficult explain it tell you but it is not possible because I do not know it. You understand the reason for these few word that I write to you. You do not know how great my love for you. Our eyes understand how much deep our love.

My heart would never tired to sing this loving hymmm but, I must close because I can't write long how you know – I am waiting a your reply, and if you please I beg you a your writing clear easy.

With all my love,
Tony

It was little wonder that none of these relationships ever fully lasted, blown away by the years of war like sea-spray or words shouted into a harsh Orcadian wind. The difficulties in these relationships can be summed up in the following verse:

AN ITALIAN POW CONTEMPLATES AN ORKNEY WOMAN

I love this woman who is to be found
living on the far side of the Sound.

Each day I work towards her, laying stone
I hope will build a dry path to her home,

allowing me to meet my loved one, greeting her with rings
fashioned out of bronze or silver, giving me the chance to sing

arias and cantatas in the tongue
that will always separate us for I do not belong

on the far side of the foreshore and she will be aware
when this labour's over, I will not settle there.

There were others who – in their own way – spoke more eloquently of their love of God. They did this in the manner of one of the figures who later came to be represented within the Chapel, St Francis of Assisi, remembering some of his words as they sought to complete their work. 'He who works with his hands is a labourer. He who works with his hands and his head is a craftsman. He who works with his hands and his head and his heart is an artist.' It was as if they had come to embody all St Francis had said, there was so much evidence of art, sweat and cunning in the work they undertook to show their love of God.

꒰ꜛ꒱

The first task is to disguise the corrugated iron walls around the chancel area, covering them with smooth panelling made from plasterboard. While the men are at work on this, Domenico utilises his own skills. At first he makes sketches, eraser in hand, to stroke out any mistakes he might make with his pencil. He dashes out lines, draws curves, trying to give greater shape to what he sees in his imagination with the sheen of soft lead he holds in his grip. He stands back from what he has created sometimes to attempt to visualise the white sheet stretched out before him. And all the time, his eraser wanes like the moon in his fingers, blurring and deleting the dark lines he has drawn, until eventually, it, too, crumbles and disappears.

There is so much art he has to draw upon, deep within the great well of his past. He remembers the Church of San Vigilio in Moena where he first went to pray, looking at the work of Valentino Roviso there. He recalls his apprenticeship with Victor Pitscheider, how much he learned from his head and hands. There was Josef Moroder-Lusenberg's painting of the Adoration with the Virgin looking down at the glory of the Child in her arms; the sculpture of the Saviour on the Cross shaped by Franz Ruggaldier; the great paintings of St Nicholas on the ceiling. From all of this, he learned the skills of trompe l'oeil that allowed the observer to believe the artist had created a three-dimensional figure. He can picture the town of Bolzano with its many frescoes painted on the cathedral walls, and the work of Andrea Mantegna he had seen in Mantua. He wants his work to remind these often-lonely men around him that despite all the modern-day Caesars they have seen, there is still a God who values peace and understanding, a Christ who died for them.

So he begins to make miracles.

He works with clay – a scarce commodity at that time, but obtained for him by Major Buckland and others in the camp. He shapes this with his fingers, giving it form and contours, transforming them into altar pillars and rails, casting them first into chalk before moulding them in concrete. The finished work is soon in place, casting its own spell on those who come like Major Buckland with additional brushes and paints for the men to use. They touch it with their hands as if they want to acquire some of the maker's artistry for their own hands, some of his skills lifted and obtained by a single touch. Its white shade contrasts with the red background which lies on the wall between the two back legs of the altar. Carefully, he paints in gold three large letters 'IHS' which represent the words, '*Iesus Hominum Salvator*' or 'Jesus the Saviour of Man'. Higher than the rest of the floor, it stands upon a rectangle of concrete.

And then, impatient for the first Mass to take place within the building, he begins work on the chancel, the centrepiece of the Chapel. On paper he sketches out rough drawings of the four evangelists, represented in their traditional ways, testing each out before he begins to paint. Matthew is the human or the angel, Mark viewed as the lion, Luke portrayed as a calf, John an eagle. Each, as Father Gioacchino reminds him, represents different aspects of the divine. 'According to some, Matthew stands for the gospel being revealed to men,' he says, 'Mark is Christ's kingly lineage. Luke stands for Christ's sacrifice. John soars like an eagle, above our human infirmity.'

He paints them on both sides of the altar. St John is a great bird, wings swirling as if emerging from a fantasist's dream, a golden halo perched behind its head. St Mark is a lion, its paw stretching out the open pages of a Bible with the Saviour's name and the word '*Pax*' writ large. '*Sanctus Lucas*' is a calf that looks upwards, the Bible on the wings that stretch out below its head. Gold predominates in the background, placed in a false alcove created and surrounded by what appears to be fine stonework. Lower down on the same walls, there are also angels in long white gowns, each one playing a musical instrument such as a zither, fiddle and trumpet.

These are powerful pictures of colour and texture, but few have time to sit back and admire the craft that has gone into their making. Others are busy too. Palumbi the smith has Domenico's plans stretched out before him. He is occupied in his own task; creating an altar gate, rood screen and two candelabra in wrought iron for the Chapel from the design his friend has created. His head is knotted in concentration, filled with enthusiasm for the work he has to do, aware that it will take four months. His concentration is all the more strange because Guiseppe Palumbi, with his Communist sympathies, is not a religious man. From Teramo originally, he worked in Philadelphia while young, following his father out to America. There he learned both English and the left-wing politics he espoused after returning to Italy. It was these views that led to him joining the army. Open in his distrust of Mussolini, he had been advised to enrol because he was told his life was in jeopardy; the Blackshirts were anxious to silence him with their fists and cudgels, using more than their customary castor oil to quieten his tongue. As one of the most fluent in English, he is aware he must rely on their hosts to play a part in all of this. His basic raw material is supplied by Balfour Beatty. Linked to their modern knowledge, he uses skills that have been around since the days of medieval craftsmen. The fantail of sparks. The short-pitched ring. The puff of bellows. The rhythms and music that allow him to create the arches designed for the curved shape and width of the Nissen hut. There is also the swirl of artistry that allows him to create the two wrought-iron gates with all their fine edgings and patterns. One has the word 'Maria', a reference to the Virgin often seen in Catholic churches, the other imitates the altar that the entire screen frames, the letters 'IHS' carved in iron.

Other men are working elsewhere, using whatever they can find to transform this Nissen hut into a holy, sacred place. Even the cans of bully beef they have been given for their rations are scraped clean and turned into candle-holders, dangling beneath the most glorious chain of stars. There is only one part of the Chapel that has to be purchased with hard cash. The gold curtains on either side of the sanctuary are bought from a firm in Exeter and paid for out of the fund set aside for the prisoners' welfare.

It is the blockships in Kirk Sound that are their greatest single resource. Previously, ships like the *Lycia* and the *Ilsenstein* provided a different bounty for the prisoners. They used to lay nets across jagged holes where the sea had cracked open hull and bow in the hope they might catch the fish that circled round the Bay of Ayre, near the Barriers. Sometimes the Italians would perch on the ships, fishing rod in hand, waiting for cod, ling, skate and mackerel to approach, making a pleasant change from – or even an addition to – the pasta they ate so frequently. There was a time when an eel was found stranded in the seaweed and brought back to the cookhouse wriggling and squirming, stretched over one of the Italians' shoulders. On another occasion a man called Bill Johnstone, who worked in the power station, instructed a former prisoner on how he might knit a small mesh net. They created their own lobster creel, baiting it before they left it beside the pier. Later, they had to find the courage to brave a lobster's pincers when the inevitable occurred, one making its way into their trap. A few scrapes and cuts meant that the experiment was rarely repeated.

However, it was not only seafood that these vessels and their surroundings provided. Covered with cement, the rocks of the shoreline provided the basis for the floor. Sometimes iron would be stripped from the boats. Wood might also be taken from there, providing the source for the tabernacle area of the Chapel. There were also the tiles around the altar. These were taken from the most peculiar source – the toilets of the *Ilsenstein*. Again, they were provided with their final sheen by Buttapasta, disguising the fact that they originally came from the urinals of the one of the wrecks nearby. On the altar, there were the four brass candlesticks made by Sergeant Primavera and two candelabra in iron created by Palumbi. Again, an act of transformation was involved in their creation, these holders of light fashioned from the carpet holders on one of the blockship's stairways.

While they were working there, men must have often come in to see their progress, shaking their heads at the sheer impossibility of a building like this being created on the Orkney landscape.

They looked on as Domenico continued, turning his attention to the centrepiece of the Chapel. As he stands behind the altar, he flicks open the top pocket of his tunic jacket, taking out a small picture contained inside. He holds his inspiration in his fingers – the illustration on the small card given to him by his mother when he was called up for the conflict: *Madonna of the Olives* by Nicolò Barabino.

Originally from Genoa, Barabino spent much of his life in Florence. He painted a fresco above one of the doorways of the Cathedral of Santa Maria del Fiore, the main cathedral in Florence and the fifth largest church in Europe, after St Peter, St Paul, Seville Cathedral and Milan Cathedral. He painted a succession of Madonna figures – *Madonna del Rosario, Madonna della Primavera*, even a *Madonna of the Lemons*. In each one, the Madonna is shown wrapped in flowing and abundant drapery, hiding most of her body as well as her head.

Domenico tries to recreate it – that picture to which he

turned again and again to find comfort during the years of war. He prays for a moment before he begins, his head reeling from a mixture of the smell of paint and turpentine in the building and the immensity of the task before him. Slowly, he raises his pencil, steeling himself to begin his work. He knows he has much to say within it. It will be his own affirmation of the value of God's peace, his own small protest against all that war has done to him and all the others in the camp. He remembers once again his playmates making their way across an open field, the shell slipping from the fingers that hold it, the smell of blood and blast blown towards him by the wind. He recalls, too, the songs that the men around him sang in their madness, words like the following echoing through city squares:

> *Temprata da mille passioni*
> *La voce d'Italia squillò:*
> *'Centurie, Coorti, Legioni*
> *In piedi che l'ora suonò!'*

The raised arm of Il Duce in Bolzano. The Victory Gate. The heat of North Africa. The desert flies of Geneifa. That long voyage north to Liverpool. The yelled insults with which they were met in Edinburgh. The journey through Aberdeen harbour. The stench of rotten fish in their nostrils. The indifference of the granite buildings all around. The cold and wet of those first few months in Orkney, when it seemed a chill had settled deep within his bones.

A Ladin phrase comes to his mind. It is one he first heard on the lips of his father when he was young. *'Empea n lumin e no maledir el scur.* Far better to light a candle than forever curse the darkness.' It strengthens him, makes him equal to the great task he has in hand.

The first pencil-stroke is made upon the wall. A curved line. A fold. The beginning of the plain white sheet that holds both the Madonna and Child in its constraints. A halo behind her head, she looks down at her offspring with great care and love, holding him between her fingers. The Child looks outward. A crown is upon his head. An olive branch is stretched out between his fingers. He offers it both to his mother and mankind, trusting that the day will come when they will both accept his gift of peace.

And around her, too, are Domenico's own inventions. He gives greater life to their forms as he continues work on the Madonna and Child, daubing his brush into the paint that the major has provided, overcome with his sense of obligation both to his art and also to the God whom men will worship in this building, a refuge from their lives of exile and imprisonment. His innovations consist of a scroll with the words '*Regina pacis ora pro nobis*' ('Queen of Peace, pray for us') wrapped around a group of cherubim who surround the Mother and Child, their dark, brown and fair heads focused on the Infant's every movement, the leaves he brandishes in his hand.

The angel on the Madonna's right hand wears a blue sheet. She also holds a scabbard in her fingers into which she sheaves her sword, setting aside the weapons of war. On the other side, there is an infant carrying a blue shield. There, Domenico reveals his own longing for his native land. It is the heraldic badge of his home town of Moena, one that might seem more suited for the island of Orkney or the town hall of Kirkwall. The crest shows a man and his boat moving out of a stormy ocean and into calm still waters.

For each man who looked at it, the image did much more than summon up an vision of Moena, far away. It expressed all that they wished for. A voyage towards a place of peace from which they had been taken by the mad and frenzied dreams of others. A return to their homeland. It was a journey that they knew would be difficult. They heard enough about the war from the pages of *Il Corriere Del Prigioniero* and from the radio about the bloodshed and suffering, of German reprisals, war refugees and battles like Monte Cassino. Some responded to these stories with silence, pretending all these brutalities were not occurring in the places where they lived. Others used the defence of humour. There was the soldier from Rome who declared that there were enough ruins in his city already. 'What on earth did a few more matter?'

They all felt strengthened by Father Gioacchino Giacobazzi's presence at the altar when Mass was celebrated in the Chapel for the first time.* A harmonium that Major Buckland had obtained was played by Sforza to accompany men like Domenico as they sang in the choir.

'*Kyrie Eleison* – Lord have mercy . . .' they sang.

'*Gloria in excelsis Deo* – Glory to God in the Heavens . . .' Their voices rang triumphantly above a fierce Orkney wind, as if they were present at the birth of Jesus.

'*Sanctus* – Holy, Holy, Holy . . .' they chanted like the angels are said to have done at the foot of the throne of God.

And then finally the Agnus Dei with its plea for mercy. 'Lamb Of God, thou takest away the sins of the world . . .'

As they sang out the words, it seemed as if there was a tremendous load lifted off their shoulders. Peace might not yet have returned to the world they had left all those many years before, setting off to the Field Of Miracles, but its coming was assured.

Yet there was still some work to be done on the Chapel. Domenico painted the windows on either side of the altar with images of the two patron saints of Italy, St Francis of Assisi and St Catherine of Siena, who catalogued the reasons for the tears of mankind. As he undertook the latter, Father Gioacchino spoke sometimes about the way she had lived: how she had helped to bring peace between the warring city-states of her native country; the words she had said to her biographer, Raymond of Capua, as she talked of her suffering and adversity. 'Build a cell inside your mind,' she had declared, 'from which you can never flee . . .'

Domenico could have thought of both his art and faith at that moment, the way they had provided him with a refuge when war

---

* Before this, he had always used a table in the Mess for the purpose.

and trouble had threatened his existence. He painted her in blue and white, her fingers clasping the crucifix as she prayed, walking across a stretch of peaceful countryside, a patchwork of green and blue. On the opposite side of the altar, St Francis of Assisi, a man who had at that time been a prisoner of war, took shape. The Church's most loved saint, he wore the traditional brown cloth and sandals of a monk, his head tonsured. A dove nestled in his fingers; another flew towards him across a stretch of blue sky.

Above these representatives of faith and devotion, a lattice of stonework and stars gleamed from a bright blue background, as if attempting to mirror the expanse of Orkney sky the Italians saw on clear nights above their heads, not shifting and electric as it was on the rare nights the Northern Lights were on display, but quiet and still. Placed there, too, was Domenico's final reminder of home. A golden dove shaped and seen from below like the one he had first glimpsed in the Church of San Vigilio in Moena. With all its promise of peace, it hovered above the heads of those of all faiths who worshipped there.

The local army chaplain, Reverend John Davis, held fortnightly services in the building for British soldiers, locals and those among the Italian soldiers who were not Catholics. Prayers were said; hymns and psalms were sung below the outstretched wings of the dove just as they had been spoken when on 23 May 1915 the parish priest had stood before Domenico's parents and warned that war was coming to their parish. In Moena, just as they did now in Lamb Holm, lips had prayed for it all to come swiftly to an end and peace to be restored to the world.

༘

It didn't look quite finished.

That was what they decided when they sang there these first weeks, the sounds and rhythms of familiar hymns like '*Adoremus Te*' or '*Salve Regina*' on their lips. The words of the latter had more effect than ever on them. They felt they were in exile, 'the poor banished children of Eve', as they stood back and looked at the sanctuary they had made. For all that the chancel was complete, the remainder of the hut with its steel ribs and semi-circular structure looked crude and unfinished, a contrast to all they had done before. Rain continued to drum on the corrugated iron of the building, distracting them from thoughts of God and prayer. The walls reminded them of their realities, how hard it was to sing the Lord's songs in a strange land when there is so much else to occupy their thoughts.

Slowly, surely, a conclusion to their dilemma was reached. It was decided that their work of transformation had to continue, that the rest of the interior had to be changed. They went to work with a will on this, the men coming together in a whirl of activity and effort to complete what had to be done. Buttapasta sweated with all his exertions once again, laying down stones from the floor of the sea nearby, smoothing it with concrete when this was finished. Major Buckland added his own efforts to the rest, managing to obtain some plasterboard, enough to line the remainder of the building in its entirety. This was fixed to a wooden framework – one that allowed the air to circulate freely between the iron on the outside and the plasterboard. The last would form the canvas for the remainder of Domenico's work within the Chapel. He picked up his paintbrush once again, faltering a little when he realised that the task would be too much for him alone.

It was at this point than another man joined him. Sergeant Pennisi from Camp 34 in Burray made his way across the Barriers to work alongside him on the nave. Pennisi had already performed a sacred task of his own, playing a major role in the creation of another chapel in Burray. Together, their brushes moved carefully up and down in slow, patient motions, right and left in their efforts to recreate the effects of brickwork on the wall. At the foot of this, they created a set of panels, outlined and surrounded by red paint, each one a perfect imitation of carved stone in a variety of shapes.

Outside there are other workers, all contributing to this frenzy of labour and love. Among them are men like Buttapasta. Again, he followed Domenico's designs as he toiled upon the outside of the Chapel, anxious now to complete the task to perfection in honour of both God and the Church. Occasionally, the men stopped and talked to one another in their energy and industry. One pointed to a red-haired Scotsman employed by Balfour Beatty and told the story of *Nasty Foxfur*, written by Sicilian author Giovanni Verga, as he passed.

'He was called Nasty Foxfur because he had red hair. And he had red hair because he was a bad, malicious boy, who gave every promise of ending up a complete villain ...'

The others chuckled but Buttapasta hardly listened. As swiftly as he could, he completed the transformation of the Nissen hut. 'On this rock,' he might have thought to himself, 'a church has been built. Let it stand.' He used all his skills to ensure that this would happen. At its centre, he created an archway supported by pillars. Gothic pinnacles, shaped with cement, were constructed to stand on either side of the building. Decorated windows added their own shade of light to the walls within.

Above the door is the head of Christ that Pennisi moulded miraculously out of cement, transforming that base material, like the woodcutter's block of wood, into something both human and divine. Crowned by thorns and shaded red, his skin is now cracked and lined by the annual onslaught of Orkney's seaborne storms. He looks like he has suffered more and more over the years for the sins of mankind. The Lamb of God gazes downward, his gaze full of compassion at the men and women who come to Lamb Holm and pass through the building's doors. Above his head there is a bell which was absent when the first photograph of the building was taken by Sergeant Major Fornasier.

Domenico corrected that by cutting a bell-like shape out of cardboard and hanging it in the gap in the Chapel's façade. A real bell, taken from a ship, was in place while the last of Buttapasta's miracles took place. The hut was encased in cement to provide it with support and resilience through the fury and fierceness of the island's weathers. And then on the doorstep, Buttapasta used tiny inlaid stone to spell out the date '1944' in Roman numerals.

At the same time, the work on the Barriers continued. Sometimes it was undone by the sea. The high tides of August 1942, for instance, caused havoc on the Barrier across Weddel Sound between Glimps Holm and Burray, breaching the ridge of bolsters that stretched 40 feet across. The depth of the water flooding through at one point was around 17 feet, running back and forth for five days. It took two days to repair this; 84 bolsters closed the gap that had been made. Sometimes it was troubled by wartime shortages, particularly of steel. At Camp 34 on Burray, for instance, they developed a new way of lifting the blocks, boring a hole through them instead of using steel bars to hoist them into place. The last to be done was the Barrier that bridged the gap between Burray and South Ronaldsay across Water Sound; a new quarry at Housebreck opened for the purpose. Finally, the task was finished. A gleaming white causeway that stretched from island to island, transforming salt into stone and cement block, ocean into land, changing, too, the lives of Orcadians, especially those who lived in Burray or South Ronaldsay. Their existences were no longer cramped and limited by the same narrow shorelines which they occupied for centuries before. The waters that lay behind them were secure too. In any future war, there was little likelihood of enemy submarines slipping into Scapa Flow to destroy one of the Royal Navy's ships. In recognition of this, the barrage balloons that had once floated above the entrance to Orkney's harbours were cleared away. London had greater need of them.

The other metamorphosis that had occurred in Orkney was also just about complete. The last of Domenico's creations is the holy water stoup. On the latter, his thumbs and fingers press out the shape of three angel heads. Folds are created for the forehead, puffed out to make cheeks. Small dry eyes stare out at the visitor. Locks of hair blow back as if the font was placed outside, shifted and stirred by a stiff Orcadian breeze. He casts their features first in chalk and then in concrete, preparing them for their position in the Chapel.

As he worked, Domenico watched most of the other Italians leaving, their departure in September 1944 overseen by people such as the landowner, P.N. Sutherland Graeme, and his daughter Alison. One of their more fluent English speakers stood up and spoke for the former prisoners, thanking their hosts for all they had done during their two-and-three-quarter years of captivity on the island. Some of them even started weeping as he spoke, no doubt aware that in comparison with so many others, they had experienced both a safe and sane war. For men like Domenico, it might have been a moment to reflect again on the fact that he could so easily have ended up in India as a prisoner with all the heat and disease that had afflicted Italian prisoners there. Instead, he had known good fortune and kindness, discovering that even in the most difficult of circumstances, human goodness could still triumph.

Some ten days later, Domenico left too, heading with around ten of his fellow countrymen to Overdale Camp in Skipton in Yorkshire to do agricultural work. With its castle and canal, it was a very different location to Orkney – more sheltered and less exposed than that northern isle with its cold sea-edged winds, the way its crops were so often bent and blighted by an occasional, unpredictable storm. He gained inspiration from this location, too, painting another church, the Holy Trinity Church in Skipton's High Street near the castle while working on the stage scenery for the local theatre. It was also a place where Domenico made friends, encountering David and Barbara Harvey who in 1959 let him know that the Orkney Chapel still existed and visited him many years later in Moena.

After that, Domenico spent ten months in Kew near London.

It is a city where it is easy to imagine him, walking around its sites and attractions, going to places like the National Gallery, where he could see the work of Andrea Mantegna hanging on its walls. He would marvel once again at the technique and skills of one of his greatest heroes, noting how he had painted *Samson and Delilah* to make it look like a cameo, carved delicately into precious stone, the great warrior's head resting in Delilah's lap while his mistress clips his hair with scissors. There is also *The Agony In The Garden* where Judas comes with the Roman soldiers to arrest the sleeping Christ. The dead tree and the vulture symbolise the death that Domenico himself has escaped from during the years of war; new foliage and the pelican show hope and promise for the future.

And then there is *The Holy Family With St John*; the young John the Baptist pointing to the Infant Christ. Watched by his parents, Jesus is standing, holding a globe and an olive branch in his hand . . .

8

... I WILL BUILD MY CHURCH

THE PAINTING OF THE DOVE

Because his world is ringed with water,
Goti draws a dove,
recalling how Noah sent one out three times,
returning to his fingers out of love

for the old man who had fed her.
Not like the raven that did not come back
but took the chance to flap
away from all who caged dark feathers tight within that ark,

And so he paints that bird upon the ceiling
so eyes can see an olive branch
caught within its beak, allowing men to dream
of days they'll brush these leaves once more with just a stretch of hands.

On the fifth day of April 2009, I attend a service in the Chapel, unaware that it is the feast day of St Vincent Ferrer, the patron saint of builders. I am conscious, however, like a few others, especially Orkney's small group of Catholics, that it is Palm Sunday, the hour that Christ entered Jerusalem on his donkey surrounded by loud and celebrating crowds, before His Crucifixion and Resurrection. In a small flotilla of cars, they drive past the wooden building where the Orkney Wine Shop is housed a short distance away from the Barrier, making their way to the Chapel for a different kind of wine – Holy Communion, the Sacrament of the Mass.

There are others, though, often and mainly Protestant, who are going to the Italian Chapel for a different reason that day. They are heading there because they are friends of a young couple, Ian and Catherine, who are about to have their baby boy baptised. Many of them feel anxious about their attendance at such an event. They are aware that the ceremonies and rituals of the Catholic Church are different from those of the church they normally attend – if, in fact, they go to any church at all. They are worried about making fools of themselves, of standing up when all the others are about to sit, whether or not they should kneel when the rest of the congregation are on their knees; yet, at the same time, they feel a strong sense of curiosity. In what way does the Catholic Church do these things differently? What words and gestures does it use to welcome a young child into their midst?

Though few of them would confess it, they are also curious about the priest who will dandle the child above the baptismal bowl. They have heard that he is 89 years old; that he is that rare phenomenon among Catholic priests, a widower with grown-up children; that he is a former Church of Scotland minister whose own grandfather was born in Main Street, Kirkwall. His name is Father Ronnie Walls* and all eyes are upon him as he emerges with alb and stole from the back room of the Chapel, wheeling himself on what seems to be a specially adapted Zimmer frame towards his place between the wrought-iron gates at the front of

---

* Sadly, Father Walls passed away in January 2010, shortly after this service took place.

the building. He stands there for a moment to catch his breath, allowing us to take in his head, bald apart from the white hair around his temples, the thick crop of his eyebrows. His eyes provide a contrast to all this, twinkling as he takes in the full congregation crammed within the walls of the building.

His voice is strong and clear. It rings around the Chapel as he explains the challenges of the ceremony that is about to occur, how the differing rituals of both Palm Sunday and a child's baptism will operate within the tight confines of these walls. He explains that he will have to make his way to the door of the church in order to bless the palms with water before wheeling down to the front again. He apologises in advance for the possibility that he might fall on top of one of the congregation on his path. People laugh at this, but a shade politely, as if they fear that such an incident might actually occur. It is only when he has completed the endeavour that we begin to relax, listening to his words from Isaiah 50 verse 4.

'The Lord God has given me a disciple's tongue. So that I may know how to speak to the weary . . .'

From Mark's gospel, he utters the same weary words that the Italian prisoners might have said when they first arrived in Orkney, seeing the bare and alien landscape that lay all around them.

'*Eloi, eloi, lama sabachthani?*'

We hear, too, how Joseph of Arimathea asked Pilate for Christ's broken body, how they rolled a stone to close his open tomb. The profession of faith is also uttered, addressed to the congregation gathered within.

'We believe in one God, the Father, the Almighty, maker of heaven and earth, of all that is, seen and unseen . . .'

Much of this is familiar to the faithful, a set of words they follow, perhaps, week upon week, year upon year, yet there is much, too, that is strange and unusual. There is the location; Mass usually occurs within the Catholic Church or, sometimes,

St Magnus Cathedral in Kirkwall. There are the strangers in their midst, who falter or remain silent through the prayers, who do not know the music to the hymns. There is also the child, wrapped up in a white shawl and nesting in its father's arms. It is to them alone that Father Walls addresses his next words: 'Could Ian and Catherine come out to join me? And bring the baby. We need a baby for the baptism.'

The two of them laugh as they step forward. Ian looks as if he couldn't quite decide whether or not to wear formal clothing for the occasion. The collar of his white shirt is upright and stiff around his neck, his jacket not quite fixed upon his shoulders, his dark hair looks uncombed. Catherine is dressed more formally. A pretty, brown-haired young woman in a blouse roughly the same shade as the sea that laps against the Barriers on one of Orkney's rare sunlit days, she blushes a little as she steps forward, glancing at the two-week-old child in her partner's arm. Ian is the one who speaks – a little nervously – when Father Walls asks for the child's name.

'Nathan Hunter Smith . . .' he says, swallowing the last word.

The priest marks the baby's chest with holy oil, crosses his forehead before inviting Ian to do the same. He speaks to both of them and the child's godparents standing on the other side of the altar, asking them if they will be responsible for the spiritual welfare of the newcomer to these isles.

'We will . . .'

After this promise, they go once again to the entrance of the church, gathering round the cement baptismal font which is near the doorway. The eyes of the congregation peer in this direction, straining to capture each last detail of what is going on. They see Ian clutching the child a little anxiously, aware of the precious nature of the burden he holds. They see Catherine smiling shyly as she stands before the door, watching Father Walls prepare for the ceremony. A few moments later and they see that grin fade from her face. Ignoring the host of cars parked outside, a visitor has arrived, pushing the door open. Muttering a soft apology, Catherine squeezes it shut with her elbow.

It is at this point my imagination takes over. Entering through the small, narrow gap the visitor has just made in the doorway, I picture the spirits of the Italian prisoners of war mingling among the others gathering around the font. They are all there – Domenico Chiocchetti, Buttapasta, Primavera, Palumbi, Loretta, De Vitto, the ones whose names are both known and unknown – clothed in the uniforms they wore throughout so many of their years in camp. Their faces bright in the glow of the Easter candle, they are smiling as they look on an event they never dreamed of observing within these walls – the baptism of a child. They utter words that would at that time have seemed a miracle, forming them on their lips. *'Il bambino . . .'*

It would not have been, of course, the first time that Domenico returned. He did so on a number of occasions before his death on 7 May 1999. The first time that he came back was as a result of a minor miracle. Unlike all the other buildings on the site, the Chapel was spared destruction. This was partly due to the persuasive powers of Thomas Alexander Thomson from St Margaret's Hope who was employed by Balfour Beatty to clear away all evidence of Camp 60. According to his daughter Margaret Hogart, who lives in Dumbarton, Thomas had formed friendships with the prisoners and, as a painter, he appreciated how much work had gone into the Chapel's creation. When he had received instructions to destroy it, he was distraught. 'My mother said he could not sleep and talked of nothing else but the Chapel. He said the Chapel was a holy place – and "we canna tak it doon".'

And so it stood – unlike its counterpart in Warebanks Camp in Burray. The creation of Giovanni Pennisi, who was responsible for the weathered head of Jesus Christ above the archway of the Lamb Holm chapel, was destroyed in 1945, falling victim like so much else to the sledgehammers and bulldozers of those charged with clearing the camp sites. The sole reminders of its existence were a few illustrations of the Camp 34 chapel. These included a postcard of its interior and a number of preliminary sketches, found in the possession of Giovanni di Blasi, one of its former prisoners. It is a sad and poignant reminder of the fact that a number of such buildings once existed, erected by prisoners of war throughout the British Isles. There was one, for instance, built by German prisoners of war in Moota on the moorland between Cockermouth and Carlisle. Another which still stands became known as the Sacred Heart in Henllan near Llandysul in Ceredigion in Wales. It was painted using clothing dye, squashed fruit and tea leaves.

The saddest of its kind was the Barony in Northgate, Dumfriesshire, where Ukrainian soldiers built their own church complete with murals and icons. Gordon Kerr, one of the guardsmen of that camp, informed me of the tragedy that followed when in early 1948 the soldiers there 'received orders that the Ukrainian POWs were to be repatriated to the USSR. The British government decreed that every POW should be given the opportunity to stay in Britain and be assimilated into the local community and a number of the wiser prisoners availed themselves of this offer. The remainder of the prisoners were duly shipped out to Odessa, in the Crimea, where on disembarkation they were promptly arrested, deemed to be traitors of the Soviet Union, and executed.'

No such dark fate affected either the Italian Chapel or the men who had worshipped there. Instead, the building remained, protected by the word of the island's owner, P.N. Sutherland Graeme, Lord Lieutenant of Orkney. In September 1944, when the majority of Italians left the island, he had vowed to them that Orcadians would cherish and care for the building.

It was something, however, that was proving difficult for them to do a decade later. More and more people were visiting Orkney every year, some of them no doubt former servicemen and women who had spent much of the war there. It was a place they no longer cursed for its remoteness, but felt a great deal of sentimentality about, singing songs like 'Lonely Scapa Flow' composed by Allie Windwick, which began with the words:

> *Do you recall, my dear, how once you walked with me*
> *Across the warm brown hills towards the shining sea . . .*

While both the statue of St George and the Chapel were now attracting thousands of visitors, there was a great deal of deterioration in the latter's condition with every passing year. Dampness, driven hard by wind, ate its way into the walls. Fingerprints smudged and stained. Some of it, particularly the lower panels, had become damaged.* There are tales, too, of names and graffiti being scrawled upon its fabric. This damage was a source of concern for Sutherland Graeme. He had been told on a number of occasions that many of the materials used for the construction of the Chapel were impossible to preserve. It was this situation that finally led in July 1958 for Father J. Ryland Whittaker, a Jesuit priest like his predecessor Father Giaoachino Giacobazzi, to urge the setting up of a preservation committee.† It was accomplished that same year with Sutherland Graeme as its president. Using the sums of money left by visitors to the Chapel, they began a series of repairs to the building.

There were ironies in the choice of a man called Stanley Hall to undertake these: before he had been invalided out of the navy and settled in Orkney, Hall had been chief petty officer in the Royal Naval Reserves, employed on the very ship that had taken Domenico Chiocchetti and his fellow prisoners north. Guarding the Italians on board, he had listened to their sighs of

---

* With the fence broken around its walls, there are tales of the sheep flocking through its doors on a few occasions, rubbing against the paint.

† A remarkable man in his own right, Father Whittaker won the Military Cross and was also a trained surgeon before he became a priest.

despair at being trapped on that vessel, their attempts at song and merriment. Perhaps he might have even have passed Domenico sitting there drawing, trying to divert himself from both his captivity and journey. Originally from Sunderland in Tyne and Wear, he was married to a native Orcadian, Isobel Wilson, who was headmistress at Scapa School, and supplemented his income by doing odd jobs around the community. Asked by the Chapel Preservation Committee to look after the building, he did what his son, now a successful hairdresser in Kirkwall, described as unskilled work around the place, trying to make sure that the building was not destroyed and ravaged by gales.

And as he laboured, news about the building's existence was spilling out from Orkney's borders, extending further and further afield, not just in the British Isles but in Europe as a whole . . .

It was the BBC that was responsible for the distance much of that news travelled. A play called *Music In Babylon* written by Bruce Stewart and broadcast on BBC Radio 4 on Sunday, 15 March 1959. It drew upon Psalm 137 for much of its inspiration; the character of Father Gioacchino Giacobazzi explaining that the words of 'By The Rivers of Babylon' were written about the Jewish people in exile being 'forced to work for a strange ruler, and it made them sad and bitter', comparing their fate to that of the prisoners. At its end, the narrator addressed the audience: 'In Kirkwall, they think highly of their Italian Church, out on Lamb Holm . . . they try to raise money to keep it in good order. They even wonder if some day they might be able to find one of the builders again, and bring him back to see the shrine he helped build in wartime to the Queen of Peace . . .'

Aided by press reports and BBC South European Department, someone who had been more than 'one of the builders' was finally found. In a special programme that was broadcast around Italy, there was, along with the words of a number of people from Orkney, a conversation with Domenico Chiocchetti who had been found in his home town of Moena, earning his living largely as a house-painter there. By then, he had left behind much of his life at war.

There was, incredibly, a chance encounter with the man who had been one of those responsible for bringing Domenico to Orkney in the first place: Winston Churchill. There, beside the narrow twisting road from Bolzano, Domenico saw Churchill with his arm outstretched. He was not gesturing in the same way he had all those years ago at the entrance to Scapa Flow, where a German submarine had slipped through, and shouting, 'These must be closed! How long will it take?' Instead, he was behaving in a way similar to how Domenico acted in the little spare time he enjoyed while not working as a house-painter or, occasionally, mountain guide: Churchill was standing at his easel and painting one of the most remarkable scenes in Domenico's homeland. Before him lay the Lake of Carezza in the Val d'Ega in the Alto Adige. Known as Lec do Ergobando or the 'Rainbow Lake' in Ladin, its brightly-hued waters reflected the startling rose-tinted shades of the Latemar, part of the Dolomites, in its depths. At sunset, it could turn fiery red, on other occasions and seasons green, blue, yellow or gold. Watching the great man paint, perhaps Domenico would have thought back to the dancing colours of the Northern Lights dipping and swirling across Orcadian sky, and of a special service in the Chapel where they played gramophone records of the bells and choir in St Peter's in Rome. He let it slip away from him. One last glimpse at the wartime leader with his fingers moving patiently up and down, the tip of his brush daubed with paint, and he was on his way. He had his home to go to; his wife Maria and his three children Letizia, Fabio and Angela were waiting for him in a much finer place even than the Grand Hotel Carezza where Churchill would no doubt sleep that night. The old ghosts of the Austro-Hungarian aristocracy, including the old emperor's tragic and unconventional wife Empress Elizabeth would be haunting the rooms around him. For all that the hotel's windows lit up with an array of electric lights, Domenico's own home with its inscription of '*Empea n lumin e no maledir el scur*' seemed to possess a much greater glow.

It was in this house that he discovered the Chapel was still standing. A souvenir booklet published about the Chapel by the *Orkney Herald* arrived in the post. It had been sent by the Harvey family in Skipton with whom he had been in correspondence since the end of the war. 'It was wonderful news,' he declared afterwards, doubtlessly having shown it to Maria, the daughter of Frederico Felicetti with whom he had spent so much time playing cards in his youth. He would smile as he thought back to his father-in-law's disdain for Fascist ideology when some of the other younger men would proclaim their fervour for Mussolini. The old man had been right. Politics was not something to get worked up about.

Some of those with whom he shared a homeland would not have agreed with that. There were German-speakers who wanted the South Tyrol to be returned to Austria after the Second World War. Organising themselves into the Südtiroler Volkspartei (People's Party of South Tyrol), they had the support of the Austrian government in arguing for self-determination for the German-speaking people. They would point out that it was Italy that had been on the 'wrong' side during the Second World War; Austria had, in fact, been the first country to suffer Hitler's aggression, the streets of Vienna echoing to the sound of German jackboots. Italians would counter that far from being victims of Hitler, some of the German-speaking people in the area had been among his most enthusiastic recruits. The cemetery of the Ancient Gries Parish Church on the outskirts of Bolzano bears testimony to that. Among its graves are those which belong to young men who fought in places like Stalingrad for the German army or those who flew in the Luftwaffe among the final days of the Third Reich. They would also recall that it was in that city that

Jews and Italian resistance fighters were imprisoned. Crimes were committed like the ones of which the 'Beast of Bolzano', Michael Seifert, was convicted in 2008.*

The tensions between the two sides increased in the last years of the 1950s and the early part of the 1960s. There were protests about the continued existence of some of the symbols remaining from the Fascist era throughout that region. The Victory Gate in Bolzano caused the German speakers particular irritation. So did the 'aluminium Duce' in Ponte Gardena, a statue of a powerful man on a horse that was said to be based on Mussolini's own features. On 6 October 1956, an explosive charge was laid at the door of the Don Bosco Oratory in Bolzano just before a meeting of young Christian Democrats was about to take place. Luckily no one was hurt. Over the next few years, the acts of rebellion escalated.

There were many incidents, such as attacks on electricity masts, army and police barracks, and rail links. This culminated in the 'Night of Fires' in June 1961 when 37 carefully co-ordinated attacks on electricity pylons were carried out; the entire city of Bolzano blacked out as a result. The work of the self-styled Liberation Committee of South Tyrol had achieved its purpose. In the world's newspapers, headlines drew attention to the unresolved tensions that still existed in that part of Italy.

Much like the Chapel he had left behind in Orkney, Domenico's peace had become tarnished. While neither the likes of Hitler nor Mussolini remained in power in Italy or Germany, Il Duce having met his quite inglorious end at the hands of the citizens of Milan in 1945, the post-war world was not without its conflicts. Yet little of it impinged on Domenico's domestic life. He was more concerned with the delights of the everyday. His children. His music. As leader of a local band, he played mandolin

---

* A Canadian citizen, he was convicted of brutally torturing and killing nine people when he worked as an SS guard in the city.

and banjo, taking the time, too, to teach his daughter Letizia how to dance the tango and the waltz. He loved opera and classical music, as well as leafing through his books of art where the works of the Renaissance masters like Botticelli and Mantegna could be found. And, of course, faith played a crucial part of his life. It felt good to sing of praising God in a landscape where there were hills to which men could lift their eyes and give thanks. It allowed him to forget the small irritations that always form a part of people's existence. Some of his neighbours would take advantage of his good nature by failing to pay the bills for his painting jobs on time. Maria would sometimes berate him for this, urging him to become tougher with these clients.

But it was generally a comfortable life that he left for a short time in March 1960. By that time, a great deal of publicity had been generated by the story of the Chapel. Articles written by Domenico and Father Gioacchino Giacobazzi appeared in the *Orkney Herald,* telling the story of how the Chapel had been built. The words heralded Domenico's arrival at Kirkwall airport on the morning of Tuesday 22 March 1960.

'Orkney,' he said, as they touched down . . .

In the beginning, he must have shivered. There were a number of reasons for that. He had, for instance, survived a journey by air that his wife had been worried about him taking – neither of them were confident air travellers. There was the once-familiar mist and rain, too, the memory of his years of imprisonment at Camp 60 taking hold. Eventually, though, he smiled, turning to the two men who had accompanied him on his journey north, Signor Ricono and Signor Finoglio. Both worked for the BBC Italian service and would remain in Kirkwall for a few days, helping to arrange Domenico's stay and preparing some recordings for broadcast on Italian radio. They would be back a few weeks later when work on the Chapel was nearly complete and a religious service would be held.

After that, he was greeted by two men from the Chapel

Preservation Committee: Father Cairns, the parish priest of Kirkwall, and Ernest Marwick. The man who had once worked in Stevenson's shop at the end of Bridge Street was now employed by the BBC in Orkney. He towered over Domenico with his black beret and duffel coat, kitted out for the rain. With a flurry of his fingers, and a stammering of speech, Domenico very quickly indicated where he wanted to go: the Chapel he had worked on all those years before.

✧

A brush was in his hand again – that tool of his trade long familiar to him from his days as an apprentice in Ortisei, from going to places like Laste or Bolzano with Vigilio Sommariva by his side, from the churches and houses of his home community of Moena and elsewhere in the fantastic landscape of the Dolomites. He thought about the last time he had used them in this building, how at the same time the men of other ranks had performed their own work of transformation, creating a road that, bright and gleaming, spanned water, bringing communities together that had long been apart.

By his side he had a new partner, Stanley Hall. He must have thought for a moment about how strangely life had turned out, how the man who had once stood over him ensuring he did not escape was now labouring alongside, helping him complete his work of faith and prayer. By sign gesture and the odd word of English he possessed, he let it be known what panels needed to be cut out, what repair work was required. The Englishman nodded and did all he could to help, eager to oblige and learn from the Italian who had come once more amongst them. He was all too aware that this was a man who had great skill in his fingers. The evidence of his work – and that of God's glory – was all around him.

There are signs of his love for his wife Maria, if the observer looks carefully enough. Less extravagant and theatrical than the blacksmith's heart, Domenico began by carving her name onto the left-hand wrought iron gate that leads to the altar. It glistened for a moment, giving him strength in the task he was about to undertake. He was back in the heart of his family, in Moena once again.*

༃

And then Domenico's fingers find their own way of praying. As they move up and down, restoring the panels to the walls where they have been battered and scraped, he thinks of his own family, Maria, Letizia, Fabio, Angela, and all he longs and wishes for them. He wants them to have an understanding of their own culture, the Ladin community that surrounds them like the mountains of the Dolomites sheltering their homes. Trying to give them that, he has taught them, for instance, to ski and learn to make their way across that dramatic landscape with all its peaks and chasms while Maria has provided them with some of the tales and legends of their past . He hopes, too, they will learn to appreciate the worth and values of others, becoming citizens too of the world, rooted in this earth yet soaring over it.

'*Deo Gratias . . .*'

He works on the heads of the Four Evangelists, the lion's head of St Mark, the dark bird of St John. As he restores their faded colours with his brush, he prays too for the people of Orkney, that they might find peace and prosperity, protection from the wars that ever since 1914 brought great ships to their harbours, filled their skies with barrage balloons. He thinks of the men and women who live in Burray, South Ronaldsay, even the Mainland of Orkney itself and asks that they be given safety from the great waves that sometimes lash across the Barriers, reminding them occasionally that they all live on separate islands and not one large whole. He hopes that they find the means to protect this building

---

* It is also possible that the inscription 'Maria' might refer to the Virgin Mary.

from the corrosive effect of wind and tide, salt and the onslaught of time, that whenever people come to the island, that they find in it a place of peace and contemplation.

'*Deo Gratia...*'

While he renews the images of the angels, his thoughts return to his own native place. He asks for peace to be granted there, for the old suspicions that exist between his neighbours in the Alto Adige or South Tyrol (whatever they might choose to call it) to fade away and disappear. He trusts that there will be enough men of goodwill among both the German and Italian communities to secure both understanding and forgiveness for all the enmity and bitterness that has gone on between them over the years. It has blighted life in that beautiful part of the world long enough.

'*Deo Gratia...*'

By the time he turns his attention to the dove and the Madonna, Queen of Peace with the Infant Jesus in her arms, there are other matters on his mind. There are the stories of the shootings in Sharpeville he has glimpsed in the Scottish newspapers: the South African police shot a crowd of black protestors, killing 69 people. As he wields his brush, he also prays for the souls of the two most powerful men in the world, President Eisenhower of the United States and Nikita Khrushchev of the Soviet Union, knowing that their armed forces possessed the power of nuclear weapons. 'Let not their quarrels result in the destruction of us all...'

'*Deo Gratia...*'

༈

On 10 April 1960, the final Sunday of Domenico's visit, there were more prayers uttered within the Chapel walls. Domenico's words and wishes were echoed by the 200 Orcadians who crowded into the building that day to take part in a service of restoration conducted by Father Whittaker. It was a ceremony repeated again throughout the length of Italy where parts of that service were broadcast on Easter Monday 1960 in a half-hour feature transmitted by 15 radio stations. As Domenico went up first to receive Holy Communion, he did so not only as an individual but also a representative of all those whose lives had been transformed by exile in a strange land, where faith had helped them to hold on to the sense of humanity that their imprisonment and suffering had been in danger of taking away.

At the altar, Father Whittaker drew his lesson from First Corinthians 3 verse 13: 'Every man's work shall be made manifest: for the day shall declare it, because it shall be revealed by fire; and the fire shall try every man's work of what sort it is . . .' The test of Domenico's work had already taken place, he continued. 'Of all the buildings clustering on Lamb Holm in wartime only two remain: this chapel and the statue of St George. All the things which catered for material needs have disappeared, but the two things which catered for spiritual needs still stand. In the heart of human beings the truest and most lasting hunger is for God.'

When the service was over, the hands of Orcadians reached out for Domenico's fingers, grasping them warmly and enthusiastically, as if they believed both the grace and skill that was present in his body could be transferred to their own by the slightest of touches. Some of them spoke about the Italian prisoners they had known, the ones who had worked on their farms or provided them with small gifts. They mispronounced names or admitted they had half-forgotten them; the space of 16 years transforming them into blurred and shadowy figures.

One farmer told the story of how Italian prisoners had performed a tug-of-war on a bull which had been stuck in a bog on their farm. 'There was a loud PLOP when they pulled the beast out. Just like a cork from a bottle! And the poor men were on their backsides in the mud.'

There were others who spoke about the whereabouts of the only Italian family who had been on the island before the war. Livio Zanrè had run a café in Kirkwall until the Italians had entered the conflict against the British. He had been interned on the Isle of Man before his release in 1943. His brother John had moved to Forres in 1936 to run a café there, and had gone back to Italy just before the war. One of the partisans in the Italian Resistance, John had been honoured by the British government for his help in assisting in the escape of Allied airmen.

It was only when he became free of all their voices the following day that Domenico had time to gather his thoughts and sit down and write a simple letter of thanks before returning once more to Moena where Maria and the children waited for him. In it, he wrote:

Dear Orcadians,

My work at the chapel is finished. In these three weeks I have done my best to give again to the little church that freshness which it had sixteen years ago.

The chapel is yours – for you to love and preserve. I take with me to Italy the remembrance of your kindness and wonderful hospitality.

I shall remember always, and my children shall learn from me to love you.

I thank the authorities of Kirkwall, the courteous preservation committee, and all those who directly or indirectly have collaborated for the success of this work and for having given me the joy of seeing again the little chapel of Lamb Holm where I, in leaving, leave a part of my heart.

Thanks also in the name of all my companions in Camp 60 who worked with me.

Good-bye dear friends of Orkney – or perhaps I should just say 'au revoir'.

Domenico Chiocchetti
Kirkwall, 11 April 1960

There have been changes since.

Some of the most momentous have occurred in the place men call either Alto Adige or South Tyrol. During the remainder of the 1960s there were several acts of terrorism, which resulted in the loss of 21 lives. However, since an agreement was signed by the man who was at that time the Austrian Secretary of State for Foreign Affairs, Kurt Waldheim, and his Italian counterpart, Aldo Moro,* there has been a slow step back to sanity within the area. A region once riven with divisions has become much less fractured, largely, it has to be said, with the assistance of the European Union. Sums in the vicinity of €96 million have been distributed for the benefit of the 83,000 residents who live in mountainous areas. As Tony Judt in his magnificent history book *Postwar* has noted, it is little wonder that the people of the Alto Adige are among the most Europhile in the continent of Europe.

The Ladin community has benefited from this funding. Among the places I visited just outside Moena is the Ladin Cultural Institute where Domenico's son Fabio works as a director. An expert on the area's culture and history, he took me around the museum that he has helped develop. An extremely modern establishment, it tells the stories of Ladin culture and myth using interactive displays. Touch a screen and creatures of mythology – like the Vivana, Salvan and Bregostena, found in that region – come alive. You can take part, too, in all the colourful ceremonies that surround a Ladin wedding or enjoy a carnival in the Fassa valley. The museum also shows the old traditions of agriculture that took place there: butter, one of their most valuable commodities, was protected from witchcraft by a six-point star carved upon a butter pat; hay was carried from the mountains on a type of cart with detachable front wheels to allow it to slide down some of the more precipitous slopes.

It is a landscape with which a number of Orcadians have become familiar over the last five decades. A group has flown from Kirkwall to Italy on a number of occasions, including the

---

* Both men became famous in world history for very different reasons: Waldheim's involvement with the Nazis was uncovered after he became UN Secretary General and Moro was kidnapped and assassinated by the far-left terrorist group the Red Brigades.

day in December 1961 when Domenico Chiocchetti was given the freedom of Moena. The council convenor, Hugh Halcro-Johnston, director of development and planning, Jeremy Baster, and the treasurer of the Chapel Preservation Committee, John Muir, watched him receive the honour. Since then, school parties have travelled in both directions, experiencing the same physical disorientation that the prisoners must have felt when they first arrived in Orkney, yet more to their delight than discomfort. The children from Moena have enjoyed the experience of being surrounded by the sea, heading out on canoes or motor-boats on these waters, relishing the sheer breadth of sky that can be seen in these parts. For the pupils of Kirkwall Grammar School, there have been entirely different pleasures. The ability to ski was not a skill seen among many of their ancestors. Nor, given the flatness of much of Orkney's landscape, was there any great need for a good head for heights.

There have also been a number of visits from the Chiocchetti family, who have journeyed to the Chapel on a several occasions through the years. Maria was first here when she and Domenico came as guests of the Chapel Preservation Committee in May 1964, receiving the honour of a reception from Kirkwall Town Council when they arrived. By that time, their lives had already been altered by the publicity surrounding the Italian Chapel. Together with a number of other artists living in Moena, Domenico was making a living creating sacred woodcarvings as well as – in the old Ladin tradition – decorating farmhouse-style furniture with floral designs. In his spare time, he also painted, exhibiting his own work.

The younger members of the Chiocchetti family – complete with wives and husbands – first visited the islands in 1970, enjoying both the warmth and welcome of the Orcadian people. Angela was a member of a choir that sang in the Chapel and also in St Magnus Cathedral. Letizia described to me how she made Orkney the beginning of a nerve-wracking journey down the twists and turns of Scotland where the people 'drive on the wrong side of the road'. In different ways, they all seem to have been inspired by their father's openness to the world. Angela adopted two children, a boy, Bijou, and a girl, Mina, from Mother Teresa's organisation in India. Letizia spent many years working in London and the Channel Islands and is now the honorary president of the Chapel Preservation Committee. Fabio, for all his love of Ladin culture, is inspired by the bossa nova, its swirling rhythms having taken him all the way to Brazil on several occasions to master its art and craft.

There have been other ways in which borders have been crossed – from reality into fiction, from the visual into other forms of art. Frank Glynn felt moved to compose a short violin piece entitled 'Domenico' after his visit to Lamb Holm one year, a work performed within the building in 2000. Two writers – Philip Paris and Kirsten McKenzie – have written novels based on the story of the Chapel. The well-known playwright Alan Plater has also spun his own drama entitled *Barriers* around the tale, one performed by the people of Orkney themselves at the St Magnus Festival in 2002 and then at the Edinburgh Festival Fringe in 2003. There have been a number of poets inspired by the location; the most prominent of these was the celebrated writer Anne Stevenson who in 1992 composed a poem called 'The Miracle of Camp 60'. In it, a former prisoner who has returned to Orkney reflects on his experience there during a time of war. A dramatic monologue, it begins with an Italian voice declaring:

> Amici d'arti, amici dei fiori, amici d'amore,
> when in our towns they told us *go fight for Il Duce,*
> we Dolomiti had to go . . .

before arriving in disgust and desolation at a place which he describes as:

> this terrible island, not one tree, not one flower.

As the poem continues, slowly a change takes place in the men, transforming their attitude to both life, work and faith. Their humanity and faith in themselves – like Pinocchio – is given back to them, having been taken away by all they have endured.

In the post-war period, the attitude of the islanders to the Barriers themselves has changed gradually. A generation has grown up that has forgotten that places like South Ronaldsay and Burray are islands, as dependent on the Churchill Barriers for their journeys as other islanders like those staying in Stronsay and North Ronaldsay are on ferries. There are occasional winter days when drivers charge across the causeway like St George about to fight the dragon, clashing with the force of wave, rock and shingle. The 'shields' that protect them from the might of Orkney's weather are smashed. Windscreens are shattered. Steel dented. Skin cut and bodies bruised and broken. Later on, after the battle is over, some of them might even attempt to blame other men for their own foolhardiness, pointing a finger in the direction of the council or the police for the blows they have suffered. Meanwhile, the concrete and stone of the Barriers stand mute and resolute; they were never supposed to carry men across water in such weather.

There have been changes to the building itself. Some of them were evident to those who drove towards the Chapel that Palm Sunday for the baptism ceremony. There is, for instance, the bitumenised waterproof covering wrapped around the building's roof, preventing wind and rain from seeping through. There is the wayside shrine that was erected beside the Chapel a year after Domenico's visit: the carving of the crucified Christ was presented as a gift from the Comune of Moena; the cross on which his body hangs and the canopy that covers his frame were made from instructions sent by Domenico to the Chapel Preservation Committee in Kirkwall. Other changes are within. A standing cross in the Chapel was, together with altar cruets of Venetian glass, a present from the mayor and community of Moena. An icon can also be seen on one wall.

Some change is quite invisible. In the mid 1990s, local artist Gary Gibson undertook work to ensure the survival of the building for many decades to come. Some of the areas where there were nails had to be treated. Panels, especially those around the windows, were damaged by water and had to be strengthened by wooden struts. There was also the dark night when the statue of St George and the dragon was vandalised, pulled down from his plinth. The scars of that occasion have now disappeared, the cracks and damage healed. In the course of attending to this, Gary discovered that the scroll of prisoners' names had been obliterated by time. Water had seeped into the bottle, rendering the list virtually illegible apart from a little design at its edge.

And then there are the gifts brought by Domenico and Maria Chiocchetti when they came to Orkney in 1964. On the wall of the Chapel are the fourteen stations of the cross, carved by hand, detailing the suffering Christ endured on mankind's behalf after the judgement by Pontius Pilate. Made from Cirmo wood, a type of pine found only in mountainous areas like the Alps, Dolomites and some parts of the Balkans, it is used for carving and making furniture in areas like the Val Gardena. From a glance, it is clear that they, too, are valuable and impressive pieces of work. Later, Maria presented the Chapel with finely embroidered cloths for use on the altar.

The plaques have, in themselves, been the reason for further alteration in the Chapel over the last few years. In early August 2014, shortly after Pope Francis gave the building a special blessing for its 70th anniversary on Sunday, 11th May, three were stolen – the ones numbered IV, VI and X. It was an event that created consternation and concern in the nation's press and media, sparking off a police search for the thieves. In October 2014, however, they were replaced. Similar plaques arrived from Moena and were fixed to the Chapel walls.

Yet, with that theft something of importance was lost, as it must have been on the earlier night when the statue was vandalised. On this occasion, though, both time and technology provided solutions. By the following March, CCTV cameras were installed, keeping an electronic eye on visitors and ensuring that nothing could be taken from the building. It also prompted other changes. By August 2015, it was announced that full-time custodians would be appointed to safeguard the Chapel. As well as collecting a modest £3 entry fee, they would also work to ensure that not too many people would cram through its doorway at one time, trailing their fingers across the artistry of Domenico Chiocchetti and the other men who worked there. It was largely this – and the effect of the passing years on the structure – that brought Antonella Papa, a restoration expert from Rome, to Lamb Holm in March 2015, around the same time that the CCTV cameras first arrived. A regular visitor to these islands, she brought her own expert eye and talents to the project. When visitors now come to the Chapel, it is as if Domenico Chiocchetti stepped out of its walls only a few moments before. The colours are bright and vivid, renewed by Antonella Papa's artistry. It is little wonder that the building continues to inspire those who come to it. Only recently I received a message from Blair Douglas, the wonderful Highland musician from Skye, to say he was completing a piece of music that had been conjured into existence by a visit to the Chapel many years before. As one who has heard some of this in advance, it seems a remarkable work, responding simultaneously to the building and the landscape to which it belongs.

When he returns to it in both this and following autumns, he will notice one more change that has taken place. Outside its door, where the old camp kitchen used to stand, there is now another Nissen hut-type building. Described as 'a facsimile of what was there in the past, but not the same' by Tommy Sinclair, a member of the Preservation committee, it is occupied by one of the two individuals who have been given work by the change in policy, selling tickets and souvenir booklets, keeping an eye on all that is going on, limiting the number of coach parties that wheel into the Chapel's car park.

Yet, as always, the greatest changes of all are those wrought by time on human life. Domenico passed away on 7 May 1999 after a period of illness. A month later, on 9 June 1999, a Memorial Requiem Mass in Thanksgiving for his life took place within the Chapel. Conducting the service was Bishop Mario Conti, then of Aberdeen,* a man who had visited Domenico in Moena and been told by his wife that 'he had left his heart' at the Chapel. In the congregation were Maria, Letizia, Fabio and Angela – listening as the words they had written in tribute to their late father were read out:

Dear Friends,

We are extremely glad to be here with you to remember our dear father Domenico. He is here among us; he is as near as he was during his life and in particular the latest year. These years have been marked by the memory of your friendship which was the best medicine for his unsteady health and an invaluable support for his spiritual well-being.

He had carefully prepared his departure from this world; his thoughts always went beyond the daily matters and, in leaving us, he said; 'Say goodbye to the friends from Orkney and all those who loved me.' He also said to our mother, 'Pray to the Madonna of Peace. She protected me on many occasions.' And she was the recipient of his last prayer and thought.

We are now here together, sharing the same pain but comforted by the same feeling of friendship, confident that the message of the Italian Chapel is a message of peace and hope that everyone can share and relate to in our daily living.

We are deeply moved and extremely grateful for the affection you showed us in this painful moment as on many occasions in the past, and on our part we will always love these places and your people as our father wished.

We embrace you all,
Family Chiocchetti

---

* Archbishop of Glasgow until 2012.

Some eight years later, on 10 July 2007, his wife Maria followed him, mourned by all who loved her, including the many visitors who arrived at their home in Moena inspired by the tales of the Chapel. These included TV producers working on a programme for STV, and journalists and writers from Britain, Italy and farther beyond, inspired by what has become known as 'The Miracle of Camp 60'. For Maria, it was often a delight to introduce visitors to the grandeur of their landscape, providing a testimony to the depths of both her and her husband's faith.

And in their passing, they have been like so many others. In 1992, for instance, a group of eight former prisoners of war, accompanied by Letizia, her husband Elio and some of their relatives, arrived at the Chapel. Men like Arduino Dibenedetti, Dino Cattellani, Coriolano Caprara were greeted by Alison Sutherland Graeme, whose father had been the landowner of Lamb Holm in the time of Camp 60, members of Orkney Islands Council and members of the Chapel Preservation Committee. A retired Italian priest, Monsignor Rossi, had travelled north from his former parish in Glasgow on this occasion to celebrate Mass in their native tongue. When the ceremony was over, Bruno Volpi, one of the former prisoners and then in his late eighties, spoke of how he had longed to make this visit for 50 years. He cried when he walked through the door, he told a reporter from the *Herald*. 'I was brought here in 1942 and I cannot believe it is still so beautiful.' Later on, he paid his own tribute to the work in the camp, noting how 'People cannot be judged by their precarious situations. Their culture, spirit and will to express themselves in creative thoughts and deeds are stronger than any limitation to freedom. This is the spirit that gave birth to the works of art on Lamb Holm.'

There were men, too, like Roberto Pendini who in 2008 returned to Orkney in his 84th year, recalling his days when, as one of the two youngest prisoners in the camp, he and his friend Guiseppe Pizzato had been called the '*Balilla del Duce*' or

'Mussolini's little officer.' In his interview, he claimed that in some ways the creation of the Chapel was 'not a religious issue. We felt that this was a memorial that was anti-war. It was a symbol against war itself.' For that reason, 'even the non-believers – the non-Christians and atheists – were willing to help.' Apparently, the old man wept as he spoke of this, tears rolling down his grizzled cheeks.

But in my imagination, I do not picture men like Roberto Pendini and Bruno Volpi as they were over the last few decades of their lives. Instead, I see them crowd round Ian and Catherine, 'the men of rustic honour' with their faces clear and unlined, eyes bright with astonishment and wonder at the sight of the baby among them – one whose innocence and purity resembles the glory of the Infant Jesus. They glance up at the painting of him too, taking in the brightness of his features, how he still stretches out an olive branch to the lonely, broken people of the world.

Their expressions are full of curiosity when they hear questions being asked – not in Latin as they were in so many of the church ceremonies of their time but in the alien tongue of English. Some are even more surprised to be able to understand them, a gift, perhaps, to these spirits on this feast day of St Vincent Ferrer.

'Do you believe and trust in God – the Father who made Heaven and Earth?'

'Do you believe and trust in his son Jesus Christ who redeemed mankind?'

And then there are the other set of words said by Father Walls as he takes and laps water over the child's head, his old fingers blessing the young life he holds within his care.

'Nathan Hunter, I baptise you in the name of the Father, Son and Holy Spirit.'

When the baptism is over, Father Walls makes his way to the front of the Chapel once again. A moment or two later, the names of saints echo within the building as they had so often within the prayers of the Italians when they spent their first winter solstice on that shore, peering through the dim light of St Lucy's Day, only to see the dark, low outlines of Orkney's islands in the distance. 'St James. St John the Baptist. St Magnus . . .' On that day, they prayed for a miracle, one that would restore their hope and faith in the grace of God and the presence of angels, trusting that some day all their certainties might return.

Today, their spirits stand within the Chapel, hearing words that are half-familiar to them as much in their rhythm as their meaning, knowing that in some ways the miracle they asked for has occurred. They stand there as the light of an April morning fills the darkness of the building, as the windows where St Francis of Assisi and St Clare are painted take on greater brightness and colour, redolent with hope. They are there, too, as the priest comes to the closing moment of the ceremony, offering them God's comfort as their reward for the work they have done upon this building, fashioning and shaping it into a place of worship. He does so with a set of words familiar to both the Catholics and Protestants in the Chapel, both living souls and these spirits of the dead.

'Our Father, who art in heaven, hallowed be thy name . . .'

AN ITALIAN POW EXPLAINS HIS FAITH

Fingers can express man's faith
in ways that people here
could never understand,
limiting their worship to
a voice or clasp
of outstretched hands,
when they could do
so much more,
showing their convictions
in ways that our Creator
has always understood,
for He knows
that in this artistry,
there is much that serves His world,
a longing for perfection found
in those who seek to live His word.

NOTES
and
ACKNOWLEDGEMENTS

Readers of this book will be aware that, as well as a strong foundation in fact, there is also a little invention in its pages. This especially applies to the conversations between men and also the thoughts, I have imagined, passing through their heads in response to various events that occurred. There has also been the use of myth and Italian (and Orcadian) folk tale, especially Carlo Collodi's *Pinocchio* and the stories of Italo Calvino. These have been included based on evidence that while they are in prisoner-of-war camps, men tell each other stories of their localities. It is a way of passing the time as well as informing their listeners something about the world they have left behind. This even extends to re-telling the plots and storylines of the various movies they have watched, whether in Italy or – as in the case of men like Palumbi – working in the United States. In this, I was inspired by Tahar Ben Jelloun's *This Blinding Absence of Light*; one of the most remarkable books I have read in recent years, it is about the imprisonment of a young student in Tazmamart Prison in Morocco after an attempt on King Hassan's life and the story-telling that helped the prisoners maintain their psychological health. This element was introduced to *And On This Rock* to add life and energy to the narrative, especially in terms of the depth of language used. With the popularity of film and TV, it seems to me that words in a work of this kind must have their own intrinsic wit and beauty, style and verve, otherwise, we might as well stare at a screen and let images tell the story. It is this, I believe, that has partly led to the blurring of the old divisions between fact and fiction in recent years.

There are two particular scenes I have invented. One of these occurs when Sergeant Major Fornasier calls Domenico Chiocchetti a 'causeway' after he has drawn the ships crowding Scapa Flow when the Italian prisoners first arrive. The other is the scene and conversation that occurs when Buckland sees the Northern Lights. While the first of these has some basis in fact, there is no evidence that any incident involving the Aurora Borealis ever occurred. It is, let me confess, pure invention. In my defence, however, let me point out that it is highly probable that the prisoners saw such a phenomenon at some time during their imprisonment in Orkney and it would have been a strange and awesome sight for anyone who came from the Mediterranean world, a unique experience. It is also the case that there are some discrepancies between the statements of Father Gioacchino Giacobazzi and Domenico Chiocchetti in the *Orkney Herald* about Major Buckland's attitude to the building of the Chapel. The former claims the major was opposed to it initially; the other states that the Welshman was extremely enthusiastic about the project, though due to some linguistic confusion, this did not appear to be the case at first. The scene that I have created here includes that misunderstanding between cultures. To add to this, I introduced another element – an island Gael present at the scene, a character whose appearance in these circumstances was not entirely unlikely. If this misleads anyone, I apologise!

Pedants and Disney-fanatics will also point out that the Italian prisoners could not possibly have seen *Pinocchio* in the Strond Cinema. Though it was made during the Second World War, its release was delayed in Europe because of the conflict.

And unlikely though it might seem, the scene involving Domenico Chiocchetti encountering his fellow artist, Winston Churchill, in the Dolomites is – in outline terms, at least – true.

Finally, I would like to thank the many people who have helped/ encouraged/inspired/provided me with hospitality in the writing and creation of this work. These include John Aberdein, Peter Macdonald (Orkney Wireless Museum), Alison Fraser, Lucy Gibbon, Sarah MacLean, David Mackie, Colin Rendall (Orkney Archives), George L. Esson, Ian and Catherine Smith, Ron Marwick, Julie Marwick, Ann Marwick, Sandy Firth, Sheena Wenham, Eileen Tait, John Nicolson, Chris Nicolson, Dorothy Rendall, Archie Wylie, Joyce Johnstone, Bertie Johnstone, Robert Hall, Cyril Parkes, Ann MacTaggart, Stuart Sim, Morag MacInnes, John McGill, Tim, Phylida and Matthew Wright, Carla Sassi (Universita di Verona), Rossella Riccobono (University of St Andrews), Angus Murray, Eileen and Graham Scott, Fiona Zeyfert (granddaughter of Lt Colonel Thomas Buckland), the staff of Shetland Library, Robert Alan Jamieson (University of Edinburgh), my school-friend and contemporary, Anna Maria Scaramuccia, Trevor Royle, Phil Cooke (University Of Strathclyde), Iona MacDonald (especially for the day she went to Bangor), Vicci Jones (Plaid Cymru office, Cardiff), Hywel Jones (National Library of Wales), Father Colin Davies (Parish priest, Lerwick), Rt Reverend Antony Moran (Bishop of Aberdeen), Archbishop Mario Conti (Archbishop of Glasgow), Alastair Carmichael MP for Orkney and Shetland and staff, Luisa Matera, Sigurd Towrie, Pam Beasant, Clare Gee, Ivan Hawick (who provided me with one of his amazing photographs of the Northern Lights), Anna Macleod (BBC Gaelic Department), Niall Mitchinson (European Commission), Gordon and Graham Kerr, Andrew Simmons (Birlinn), Anna Mazzel (RAI Producer, Bolzano – Ladin Department), Maggie Priest, Andrew, Sarah and Maria, and the Chiocchetti family (Fabio, Angela, Letizia) who made me so welcome during my stay in Bolzano, Letizia's husband, Elio Fonti* (who acted as my chauffeur), Tom Muir

---

* In his working life, Elio was a journalist. The 'Father of the Chapel' in another sense of the word, he was a trade unionist in the newspaper industry.

(Orkney Museum), John Muir (Chapel Preservation Committee) who assisted me in Orkney, and finally Anita Joseph and Deborah Carr for their help in the creation of this book.

It should be noted that a number of people have passed away since its initial publication. My sympathy goes to all those who mourn their loss.

The fact is that in any work of this kind there are many fingers tapping the writer's keyboard, playing a vital role in its construction. I fear I am bound to forget the names of some of the people who have helped me in this task and apologise profusely for my amnesia.

In my other tongue, *taing dhaibh uile*. Your kindness is much appreciated.

Donald S. Murray

July 2010

BIBLIOGRAPHY

Barzini, Luigi – *The Italians* (Hamish Hamilton, 1964)

Bierman, John, and Smith, Colin – *Alamein – War Without Hate* (Viking, 2002)

Bosworth, R.J.B. – *Mussolini* (Arnold, 2002)

Bosworth, R.J.B. – *Mussolini's Italy – Life under the Dictatorship* (Allen Lane, 2005)

Calvino, Italo – *Italian Folk Tales*, translated by George Martin (Penguin Books, 1982)

Chiocchetti, Fabio – *Enchanted Dolomites – Folktales from the Fassa Valley* (Ladin Cultural Institute, 2002)

Collodi, Carlo – *Pinocchio* (two different editions: translated by Geoffrey Brock, New York Review of Books, 2009; translated by M.A. Murray, Nelson Classics, 1939)

Cormack, Alastair and Anne – *Bolsters, Blocks and Barriers* (Orkney View, Orkney, 1992)

Cowell, John – *Bangor: A Pictorial History*, Volume 2 (John Cowell, 1997)

Dixon, Andrew Graham – *The Renaissance* (University of California Press, 2000)

Drysdale, Helen – *Mother Tongues: Travels Through Tribal Europe* (Picador, 2001)

Duggan, Christopher – *The Force of Destiny: A History of Italy since 1796* (Allen Lane, 2007)

Eighth Army: From the Western Desert to the Alps – Robin Neillands (John Murray, 2004)

Esson, G.L. – *Gas Masks and Ration Books* (Orkney Publication)

Gilbert, Martin – *Finest Hour – Winston Churchill 1939–41* (Heinemann, 1983)

'Guide to the Ladin Museum of Fassa' (Ladin Cultural Institute, 2005)

Hazell, Howard – *The Orcadian Book of the Twentieth Century* (Orcadian, 2000)

The Herald

Hibbert, Christopher – *Benito Mussolini* (Longman, 1962)

Holland, James – *Italy's Sorrow – A Year of War 1944–45* (Harper Press, 2008)

Holland, James – *Together We Stand* (HarperCollins, 2005)

The Independent

Jelloun, Tahar Ben – *This Blinding Absence of Light* (Penguin, 2005)

Jenkins, Roy – *Churchill* (MacMillan, 2001)

Judt, Tony – *Post-War* (Penguin, 2006)

Korganoff, Alexandre – *The Phantom Of Scapa Flow*, translated by W. and D.M. Strachan (1974)

Lamb, Gregor – *Sky Over Scapa 1939–1945* (Byrgisey, 1991)

MacDonald, James – *Churchill's Prisoners – The Italians in Orkney 1942–1944* (Orkney Wireless Museum, 1987)

Manchester, William – *The Caged Lion* (Michael Joseph Ltd, 1988)

McGuirk, Dal – *Rommel's Army in Africa* (Hutchinson, 1987)

McKendrick, Jamie, ed. – *The Faber Book of 20th-Century Italian Poems* (Faber and Faber, 2004)

Morante, Elsa – *History: A Novel*, translated by William Weaver (Penguin Classics, 2001)

Muir, Tom – *The Mermaid Bride and other Orkney Folk Tales* (Orcadian, 1998)

O'Connor, Desmond – 'From Tobruk to Clare: the experiences of the Italian prisoner of war, Luigi Bortolotti, 1941–1946' (Flinders University, Adelaide)Available online at ehlt. flinders.edu.au/deptlang/fulgor/volume113/papers/fulgor_vii3_oconnor.pdf

Orcadian, The

Orkney Herald

'Orkney's Italian Chapel', Chapel booklet

Paris, Philip – *Orkney's Italian Chapel* (Black and White, 2010)

Paris, Philip – *The Italian Chapel* (Black and White 2009)

Plater, Alan – *Barriers* (2001)

Press and Journal

Smith, Denis Mack – *Mussolini* (Weidenfield and Nicolson, 1981)

Spark, Muriel – *The Prime of Miss Jean Brodie* (Macmillan, 1961)

Sponza, Lucio – *Divided Loyalties* (Peter Lang, 2000)

Steininger, Rolf – *South Tyrol – A Minority Culture of the Twentieth Century* (Transaction Publications, 2003)

Thompson, Mark – *The White War* (Faber and Faber, 2008)

Turner, David – *Last Dawn* (Argyll, 2008)

Verga, Giovanni – *Life in the Country* (Hesperus, 2003)

Vidale, Denis – 'I Was A Loo's Digger: the memory of Italian PoWs in Scotland in WWII' (*History Scotland*, vol. 9, no. 2 March/April 2009)

Weaver, H.J. – *Nightmare At Scapa Flow* (Birlinn, 2008)

Zweig, Stefan – *The Post Office Girl*, ts. J. Rotenberg (Sort of Books, 2009)

The poems which appear at chapter openings are by the author
Various documents were obtained through Orkney Archives.

tuttofassa.stepdev.org/engladinia.htm

www.uoc.edu/euromosaic/web/document/ladi/an/i1/i1.html

www.ansa.it/opencms/export/site/notizie/rubriche/daassociare/visualizza_new.html_990569095.html